A M E R I C A N
P R O F I L E S

Naturalists, Conservationists, and Environmentalists

■

Eileen Lucas

Facts On File®

AN INFOBASE HOLDINGS COMPANY

BUT 2-25-99 19.95

Copy 1

Naturalists, Conservationists, and Environmentalists

Facts On File, Inc.
460 Park Avenue South
New York NY 10016

Library of Congress Cataloging-in-Publication Data .
Lucas, Eileen.
    Naturalists, conservationists, and environmentalists / Eileen Lucas.
        p. cm. — (American profiles)
    Includes bibliographical references and index.
    ISBN 0-8160-2919-9
    1. Naturalists—United States—Biography—Juvenile literature.
    2. Conservationists—United States—Biography—Juvenile literature.
    3. Environmentalists—United States—Biography—Juvenile literature.
    [1. Naturalists. 2. Conservationists. 3. Environmentalists.]
    I. Title. II. Series: American profiles (Facts On File, Inc.)
    QH26.L83 1994
    508'.902'273—dc20
    [B]   93–46070

Facts On File books are available at special discounts when purchased in bulk quantities for businesses, associations, institutions or sales promotions. Please call our Special Sales Department in New York at 212/683-2244 or 800/322-8755.

Series interior by Ron Monteleone
Cover design by F. C. Pusterla Design
Printed in the United States of America

MV FOF 10 9 8 7 6 5 4 3 2 1

This book is printed on acid-free paper.

Contents

Acknowledgments

I wish to thank all of the people who helped me with information and photographs for this book, including The Mill Grove Audubon Wildlife Sanctuary, The Woodstock, Vermont, Historical Society, Charles and Nina Leopold Bradley and the Leopold Memorial Reserve, The University of Wisconsin Arboretum, Margaret Murie, The Teton Science School, The Snake River Institute, Bonnie Kreps and the Mardy Murie Film Project, The Friends of the Everglades, The South Florida Water Management District, Shirley Briggs and the Rachel Carson Council, David Brower, Jimmy Langman and Earth Island Institute, Gaylord Nelson, the Wisconsin Conservation Hall of Fame, the National Park Service, and B&B Publishing. There are pictures in this book taken by my father when I was a little girl, and pictures taken by my husband, just this year. I hope that these places will still be here for my children to photograph for their children.

Introduction

America has often been called "the land of opportunity." Oftentimes that has even included the opportunity to achieve financial success at the expense of the land itself. This book is about people who, in one way or another, spoke up for the land.

They lived different lives in different places in different times. John James Audubon, born in the French colony of Saint-Domingue in 1785, lived in Kentucky as an adult when that was the western frontier. John Muir, born in Scotland in 1838, was a college student in Wisconsin when the Civil War broke out. George Perkins Marsh witnessed the erosion of land due to human mismanagement in Vermont in the early 1800s; Aldo Leopold saw the same thing happen in Arizona a century later. Olaus Murie and Rachel Carson both spent years working for the U.S. government as biologists, but his specialty was large mammals and he worked in the field in Alaska and Wyoming, while her specialty was marine life, and she worked mostly in Washington, D.C. and along the Atlantic coast. While Margaret and Olaus Murie were exploring the Arctic tundra on their honeymoon in 1924, Marjory Stoneman Douglas was writing short stories about Florida in Miami. As this book goes to press, Marjory Stoneman Douglas is 104 years old and still fighting for the Everglades. Margaret Murie, David Brower, and Gaylord Nelson are also still actively involved in conservation.

All of these individuals were drawn to the natural world as they grew up. As adults, all of them pondered the question of the relationship between people and nature. Each of them believed that being able to be outside, in a place that is wild and free, is important, and that it is a right we owe to future generations.

When the first white settlers came to America from Europe, they were greeted by thick forests and swampy marshlands teeming with life. Various groups of Native Americans had farmed and hunted in this land for centuries with little negative impact. They believed that animals, plants, and people were all children of the Earth and were all related. An individual could use various plants and animals and pieces of land, but they were not his or hers to own.

The colonists, on the other hand, generally saw the wilderness of the New World as something evil, something to be conquered and controlled. And there seemed to be so much land that there was no need to be careful with any of it. As a young man who had

From the time of John Muir to the present, "Save the Redwoods" has been among the most urgent rallying cries of the conservation movement. These trees are part of Stout Grove in Jedediah Smith Redwoods State Park.
(Courtesy of National Park Service, HFC Historic Collection)

Introduction

grown up on a farm in colonial Virginia, Thomas Jefferson once wrote, "The indifferent state of agriculture among us does not proceed from a want of knowledge merely; it is from our having such quantities of land to waste as we please."

Though Thomas Jefferson would become more interested in land and soil preservation as he grew older, this attitude, that there was land enough to waste, would dominate the thinking of many Americans for years to come. By the time the colonies became the United States, many of the plants and animals that had been so abundant a century before had become rare, and some were already extinct.

This trend continued as settlers pushed westward over the Appalachian Mountains. The government had determined that these vast stretches of "unoccupied" land (they didn't count Indians) were owned by the nation on behalf of all the people. Thus it could be sold to enrich the national treasury. Individual farmers cleared plots of land and claimed it for themselves. Huge tracts were sold to speculators who made fortunes subdividing parcels and selling the smaller pieces to farmers, miners, loggers, and other interests. Few people seemed to care how badly the land was treated because there was always so much more.

But there were a few, almost from the start, who tried to raise a flag of caution. In the 1820s and 1830s, John James Audubon, painter and naturalist, noted that destruction of forests was causing a decline in wildlife. In 1864, George Perkins Marsh published *Man and Nature,* in which he decried the abuse of land that had gone on for many centuries in other parts of the world, and which was destroying the American environment.

In that same year, President Abraham Lincoln signed a measure to set aside Yosemite Valley for the use of the American public, making it the first scenic reserve protected for its beauty. When John Muir arrived there in 1868, he worried about grazing, mining, and lumbering that threatened the beauty of the valley and the surrounding mountains. He worked for the creation of Yosemite National Park, which would eventually include the valley, and numerous other national parks. He was a preservationist who believed that some places needed to be preserved, just as they were, as sanctuaries for the human spirit. This was in contrast to his contemporary, Gifford Pinchot, for whom conservation meant "wise use." They represented a dichotomy in the thinking of conservationists that continues to this day, but both agreed that the waste and destruction of forests and other natural resources had to be stopped. Fortunately, so did President Theodore Roosevelt, who had previously founded the Boone and Crockett Club, one of the first wildlife groups to work for the protection of certain game animals and their habitats. In 1908 Roosevelt called for a White House Conference on Conservation, one of the first public uses of the term.

Despite the work of Muir and other conservationists, the "Great Raid" on American resources that had begun after the Civil War continued into the 1900s. A dramatic surge in industrialization and urban growth had taken a costly toll on the environment. When the stock market crashed in 1929, it was more than just the economy that was bankrupt. Much of the American environment was down and out as well. In many places the land had been so terribly abused by overgrazing, strip-mining, clear-cutting, and careless farming, that now tons of American topsoil blew away in the wind, literally blotting out the sun for hundreds of miles across the Southwest and Midwest of the nation.

As fate would have it, there was another Roosevelt in the White House, and Franklin cared as much about the land as Theodore had. He understood that restoring the land was a key component in renewing the spirit of the people and revitalizing the economy. He listened to men like Aldo Leopold, the first professor of game management at the University of Wisconsin, who spoke of a land ethic, an attitude that required people to take responsibility for the land they depended on for life.

But soon the nation would be distracted by World War II, and after that we were all caught up with the rush to live in the "modern age." The public was told that DDT and other chemicals were going to win the war on insects and we would never be bothered by such pests again. The world was going to be a wonderful place.

There would be costs, however, though no one wanted to talk about that. Fortunately, a biologist named Rachel Carson spoke up. She wrote a book called *Silent Spring*, in which she warned us that we could not ignore the basic biological principles that connected all living things. She did not discover the chain of life; Aldo Leopold had spoken of it, as had George Perkins Marsh one hundred years before. But it was in reading *Silent Spring* that many people first became truly impressed with how interconnected all life forms are, including human beings.

Many people have called the publication of *Silent Spring* the beginning of the environmental revolution, the beginning of the

Introduction

Muir Woods. This stand of redwoods was given to the people of the United States by Congressman William Kent in 1907. He asked that it be named in honor of John Muir. It is said that of all living things, Muir liked trees, especially big, old trees, best.
(Courtesy of National Park Service, photo by George Grant)

education of the general public on its need to ask questions about what was happening to our environment. It led to the establishment of the Environmental Protection Agency to control sources of pollution. It led to people getting actively involved in fighting pollution, joining such groups as the Sierra Club, led by David Brower in the 1950s and 1960s, and Friends of the Earth, founded by Brower in 1969, and in participating in the first Earth Day celebration, organized by Gaylord Nelson, on April 22, 1970.

At the same time, a dramatic event occurred that would change for all time the way many people looked at the Earth. On July 20, 1969, American astronauts walked on the moon. When they sent back photos of the Earth from space, people noticed how beautiful and blue the planet looked from space, where none of the pollution could be seen. None of the borders between nations could be seen either, and people realized that environmental problems don't stay within a nation's borders; they are global.

All these events together were signals that environmentalism was developing as conservationism widened its scope of concerns. It was a movement beyond a concern for resource management to concern for the total environment. It did not negate the things that naturalists and conservationists had been saying all along. It simply put them in reference to a bigger picture.

One of the early landmarks in environmentalism was the 1972 United Nations Conference on the Human Environment, popularly known as the Earth Summit, held in Stockholm, Sweden. It was a recognition by one of the world's greatest humanitarian organizations, and thus by many nations of the world, that solving the problems of the environment was clearly connected to solving other human problems. And it reinforced the idea that these concerns were global in nature.

Twenty years later the scene was different, but the concerns were the same. In 1992 the venue was Rio de Janeiro, Brazil, and the event was the United Nations Conference on the Environment. Whereas the focus in 1972 had been to point out major global environmental problems, in 1992 the question was, "Can we save the planet?" The answer to that question remains to be seen. But one thing is certain. We have the words of many great naturalists, conservationists, and environmentalists to guide us. It is now up to us to carry on the work.

John James Audubon: Frontier Naturalist

A self-portrait of John James Audubon painted in 1822.
(Courtesy of National Park Service, HFC Historic Collection)

Spring had come to the Pennsylvania countryside. On a farm known as Mill Grove, a young Frenchman, newly arrived in America, set out to explore a wild section of the estate. Coming upon the wooded shores of Perkiomen Creek, he discovered a rock cave with many small ledges both inside and out. On one of the outside ledges was an abandoned bird's nest.

Inside the cave was room for the young man, 19-year-old John James Audubon, to sit. This immediately became his favorite hideaway, a place to come to sometimes with a book to read, sometimes with pencils and paper for sketching, sometimes just to think and dream.

One morning the phoebes (small, dull-colored birds) who had lived in the nest outside returned from their winter territory. John James saw that they were frightened to find him near their old nest, so he left quickly. When he returned the next morning, he saw that they had built a new nest in the cave. He continued to visit the cave often, and the phoebes came to know him well enough to stop being frightened. In a few weeks he discovered eggs in their nest and watched with joy as the eggs hatched and the young birds learned to fly. Before the phoebes flew south in the fall, he tied strings to the hatchlings legs so that he could tell if the same birds returned in the spring.

This was the fall of 1804, and may very well have been the first "banding" of birds in North America. It was also one of the first times that John James Audubon went beyond collecting birds' eggs and nests and began to actually study birds. That study led to some of the most beautiful paintings of American birds ever made. It was also the beginning of a deep and abiding appreciation for birds and their habitats that would reach well beyond the life of the painter.

John James Audubon was born in the Caribbean island colony of Saint-Domingue, on April 26, 1785, to a French naval officer and plantation owner, Jean Audubon, and his mistress, Mademoiselle Rabine. His mother died while John James was still an infant, but she was followed by other mistresses, and at least one other child, Rosa, born in 1787.

When John James was about six years old, his father returned to France, bringing his illegitimate children with him. His wife, Anne, who had remained in France all these years, accepted the children immediately and loved them as if they were her own. In fact, she spoiled John James so badly while his father was away on business that the boy grew conceited and lazy.

John James Audubon

John James would later write of Anne:

She was devotedly attached to me, far too much for my own good. [She allowed me] to do much as I pleased, and instead of applying closely to my studies, I preferred associating with boys who were more fond of going in search of birds' eggs, fishing, or shooting. My little basket went with me, filled with good eatables, and when I returned home, it was replenished with what I called curiosities, such as birds' nests, birds' eggs, curious lichens, flowers of all sorts, and even pebbles.

Besides collecting things of nature, John James enjoyed drawing pictures of the things he found. Everyone but Anne was quick to point out that his pictures weren't very good, but John James was satisfied that a head and tail and two sticks for legs satisfactorily represented a bird.

Meanwhile, Napoleon was gathering an imperial army, and John James was now 18. So in 1803, to save John James from the draft, Jean Audubon decided to send him to a farm he owned in America.

A recent photo of Mill Grove, Audubon's first home in America. Today the Mill Grove Estate is maintained as an Audubon Wildlife Sanctuary, a living memorial to the work of the naturalist and painter.
(Courtesy of Audubon Wildlife Sanctuary)

Once settled at Mill Grove, his father's estate in Pennsylvania, John James was pretty much on his own. There was a tenant farmer to look after the property while the farmer's wife took care of the household. Audubon became friends with a neighboring family, the Bakewells, recently emigrated from England. He quickly fell in love with Lucy Bakewell and began courting her.

Most of his time, though, he spent tramping around the farm, exploring, hunting, fishing, and collecting. It was on one of these "exploring expeditions" that he discovered the phoebes' cave. He spent a great deal of time there, closely observing the birds, and writing about them in his journal.

Without realizing it, the boy who had avoided study was becoming a student of bird behavior. Late at night he sat in his room sketching, trying to capture the beauty of living things on paper. But always he failed miserably. He could not make his birds look anything like they had in life.

He tried hanging dead birds upside down with their wings spread so that he could see more of the detail, but the birds in his drawings were stiff and lifeless. He tried sketching the phoebes and other birds as they flew around him outside. But they moved too quickly to copy well, and still his renderings were no where near as beautiful as the real things. There were then no field guides or other books he could turn to, or public museums to visit, and he almost despaired of ever improving his technique.

Then one day he had the idea of using wire to hold his dead specimens of birds in lifelike positions. This was a turning point in his efforts, and almost immediately his artwork began to improve.

In 1805 he returned briefly to France to discuss the affairs of the farm and his love for Lucy Bakewell with his father. But the threat of conscription was still very real, so he returned to America with Ferdinand Rozier, a young man who was to be his business partner.

Back at Mill Grove, Audubon returned to courting Lucy and collecting natural objects. His pictures of birds began to show some maturity and personal style. He had learned to see and convey details, and frequently included eggs in the drawings to complete them. He was pleased to see that some of the phoebes that returned to the farm that spring wore the threads he had attached to their legs.

In 1807, Audubon and Rozier decided to try their luck as shopkeepers on the frontier. They traveled by coach and horse across Pennsylvania to Pittsburgh, and from there headed by flatboat down the Ohio River to Kentucky.

The partners set up shop in the frontier town of Louisville. Sure that his fortune was just around the corner, Audubon went back to Pennsylvania and married Lucy on April 5, 1808. He brought her back to Louisville, where they lived in an inn known as the Indian Queen. This was not exactly the life of comfort Lucy had grown up in, but John James convinced her that soon things would be better.

But instead of working hard at the shop to provide for his wife, Audubon left most of the work to Rozier while he headed for the woods to hunt deer and squirrel and fowl. Even when he and Lucy became parents of a son, Victor, on June 12, 1809, Audubon continued to spend much of his time in the woods. He was able to keep his family fed, but he did not contribute much effort to the business.

He did greatly increase his portfolio of bird pictures, accumulating some 200 life-sized drawings. Though they were not yet of the superior quality of his later paintings, they were much better than his early efforts. His years of collecting, mounting, and studying live specimens had given him an eye for detail, and the many hours spent sketching and redrawing were beginning to pay off in technique. While his wife and his partner clamored for a share of his time (Lucy wrote to her sister, "I have a rival in every bird"), Audubon's passion for his hobby only grew.

One day a man named Alexander Wilson came to visit. Wilson was one of America's first ornithologists, the scientific study of birds being brand new in America. Hearing that Audubon was interested in birds, he wondered if the storekeeper would become a subscriber to his recently published book, *American Ornithology*. (The book would be published in a series of volumes, each of which would be paid for as received.) Audubon was tempted, but money was tight, and anyway he already had pictures that he'd drawn himself of many of the birds shown in the book. In fact, he had pictures of many birds that weren't even shown in the book, and some of his paintings were much better than Wilson's.

Wilson soon went on his way without Audubon's subscription. But this meeting of bird watchers was important for Audubon. It introduced him to the possibility that something he regarded as a hobby (observing and drawing birds) could become a life's work. He began carrying his sketchbook with him more often on his frequent hunting trips.

The firm of Audubon and Rozier moved their shop downriver a few miles to the town of Henderson, and then to the town of St. Genevieve on the Mississippi River, a little north of its junction with the Ohio River. At that point they parted ways, and Audubon returned to Henderson.

There he went into business with Lucy's brother Thomas, but Audubon and Bakewell never seemed to have as much capital as expenses, and Audubon never seemed to have much motivation for the day-to-day grind of business.

In November 1812, a second son, John Woodhouse Audubon, was born, but still Audubon continued to wander the woods with rifle and sketchbook in hand. No matter how much he loved his family and dreamed of providing for them, he found the call of the wilderness irresistible.

In 1819 too many debts came due in an unforgiving economy, and Audubon was forced to declare himself bankrupt. He moved his family to Louisville were he was able to earn a little money painting portraits. At least his skills as an artist had progressed enough to keep them from starving. When that job ran out they moved to Cincinnati. There he stuffed animals for a museum and did a little teaching on the side.

In June 1820, Audubon listened to a speech given by the museum's curator about the paths used by birds for migration, called flyways. The speaker indicated that although the flyways of the Atlantic coast had been studied by ornithologists such as Alexander Wilson, there was a need for information about the birds of "the west," those that used the Mississippi River flyway.

For the first time, Audubon gave serious thought to studying and drawing the birds of frontier America with the intent to publish his pictures. He assumed that Wilson had been successful in earning money from his book because he had become famous. In fact, Wilson had died penniless in 1813. But not knowing this, Audubon decided to publish a complete collection of all the birds of America. He would paint them life-sized in natural positions in their native environment.

He left Cincinnati on October 12, 1820, to collect specimens of birds he had not yet drawn. He was accompanied by a teenage boy named Joseph Mason who would serve as assistant and apprentice. They were given a reduced fare on the flatboat they rode in exchange for hunting services.

Audubon set himself the task of searching out and examining birds that had not been named or described for the scientific

6

John James Audubon

community, as well as commonly known birds. Because of this he made some mistakes. He thought there were two kinds of eagles, but the "new" eagle he "discovered" was really an immature form of the already well-known bald eagle.

Audubon was excited to be on such a mission. He wrote in his journal, "my talents are to be my support and my enthusiasm my guide in my difficulties." But at the same time he was depressed that he was so poor. As the flatboat passed Louisville and Henderson, it upset him to think that he had so little material wealth to show for all his years in America.

On December 23 he was able to shoot and retrieve a pelican to use as a specimen for drawing. On Christmas day the captain of the flatboat presented him with a duck hawk, another bird that Audubon was happy to add to his collection. Though he missed his family and was lonely and worried about the future, he was encouraged by the number of new birds he'd been able to sketch since leaving Cincinnati.

Audubon finally arrived in New Orleans in January 1821. He was able to earn enough to eat by drawing portraits and teaching art, but he had very little to send to Lucy and the boys. Still he continued to observe, collect, and draw birds. In his journal he wrote:

> *Monday 19th February 1821. The weather beautiful, clear and warm. . . . Saw this Morning Three Immense flocks of Bank Swallows that past over Me with the Rapidity of a Storm, going Northeast, their Cry was heard distinctly, and I knew them first by the Noise they made in the air coming from behind Me. . . . I was much pleased to see these arbingers of Spring but Where could they be moving so rapidly at this early Season I am quite at a Loss to think.*

In December 1821, he was joined by Lucy and the boys, and in 1822 they moved with him to Natchez. As an educated Englishwoman, Lucy had no trouble finding work as a governess and teacher, and it was her income that enabled them to get by. Audubon had a more difficult time earning a living as he continued to study and paint birds. "Unfortunately, naturalists are obliged to eat," he wrote in his journal, so he turned to portrait painting and teaching French, dance, and art as a means of living. In October 1823, he headed up the Ohio again, his destination this time, Philadelphia, his hope, to find employment and a publisher for his book.

Though he received favorable comments on his pictures, he soon antagonized many influential people, and it became clear that he would not find a publisher there. He moved on to New York, where the Lyceum of Natural History said of him:

This gentleman, with an enthusiasm equalled by that of our late lamented Wilson has devoted nearly twenty years to American Ornithology. He has followed the birds into their most secret haunts, and traversed the United States in almost every direction. To the learnings of a naturalist, he unites the skill of an artist, and his magnificent collection of drawings, representing four hundred species, excels anything of the kind in this country and has probably never been surpassed in Europe.

But still he could not find a publisher. He finally returned to Cincinnati, where he had to borrow money for steamboat passage to Louisville. Unable to afford a cabin berth, he slept on a pile of wood shavings on deck. He was truly destitute.

He eventually made his way back to Lucy at the plantation in Louisiana where she was working as a governess. He had decided that he would seek a publisher in England. He spent most of the next year working on his pictures while he and Lucy saved as much of their earnings as possible to fund his trip to Europe.

He was 41 when he left for England in the spring of 1826. Upon arriving in Liverpool, he was fortunate to make some influential friends, and was able to arrange a public exhibition for his pictures at the Royal Institution there.

He decided to draw attention to himself and his paintings by dressing the part of the American woodsman, with rough leather clothes and hair worn long and loose. He loved to tell stories of his wilderness adventures, which were (as such stories often are) part truth and part pure imagination. He was able to entertain people at parties with quick sketches of themselves and soon became quite popular.

Moving on to Edinburgh, Scotland, in the fall of 1826, he met the engraver, W. H. Lizars, who was extremely impressed with his paintings. Audubon's dream of publishing his work was realized when Lizars promised to engrave and publish the pictures, five at a time. Audubon would sell subscriptions for these five-unit sets, called numbers, just as Wilson had done so many years before.

Together Lizars and Audubon decided that the pictures should be published, as they were drawn, in life size, which would make the book very big and very expensive, but also very unique. The book would be called *The Birds of America.*

Audubon concentrated on drawing every aspect of the birds, from their colors to their shapes, as accurately as possible. But he also wanted to show them in realistic positions and natural settings. He felt that some pictures of birds were scientifically

The wild turkey, as painted by John James Audubon for his book The Birds of America. *By Audubon's day, these birds were already far less common than they had been when Europeans first arrived in America.*
(Courtesy of National Park Service, HFC Historic Collection)

accurate, and others were beautiful. He wanted his to be both, and this is what would set his book apart.

Late in November 1826, the first printing was produced. This included the wild turkey cock, the yellow-billed cuckoo, the pro-thonotary warbler, the purple finch, and the Canada warbler. Each painting was beautifully drawn and colored and printed, lifelike and lifesized.

Then Audubon set out on the grueling work of selling subscriptions. Traveling through the English countryside, he'd rent a room, deliver his letters of introduction and invitations for people to see the first five pictures of the book. Then he'd wait for them to come. When the subscriptions began to trickle in, Audubon was heartened and encouraged. He continued to work at completing additional paintings, supervising the production of engravings, and selling subscriptions. It was a constant battle to keep earnings ahead of expenses.

Slowly he began to gain an international reputation as a painter. In 1828, he received an outstanding review of his book by the renowned French naturalist Baron Georges Cuvier. Cuvier called the work "one of the finest books on birds that he had ever seen."

Audubon dreamed of becoming financially stable enough to send for Lucy and the boys, who were now almost grown themselves. He was in fact more wealthy and respected than he had ever been in America, but Lucy, so far away in Louisiana, found it hard to believe that it could last. She was determined to stay right where she was for the time being.

In April 1829, Audubon made the journey across the Atlantic to America, planning to collect more specimens and sketches to take back to England for further numbers of the book. In November, he traveled to Louisiana to see Lucy and to convince her to come with him to England. Together they traveled back East, retracing the route they'd taken as newlyweds when she'd first gone west with him. The memories of the difficult times she'd endured with him since then must have been eased by the reception they were given now at parties in the East, including being introduced to President Andrew Jackson.

Back in England, Audubon returned to the work of painting and selling. In addition, he was now writing a book of descriptions of the birds and their behaviors to compliment his pictures. It would be called *Ornithological Biography* and would also include a number of wilderness adventure anecdotes. With the help of an editor who understood the English language better than Audubon and also knew a little about birds, he prepared life histories of about 500 different kinds of birds. The first volume of *Ornithological Biography* was published in April 1831.

In one entry, that of the wild turkey, a bird that had once been extremely abundant across America but which was already becoming rare by Audubon's day, he described how he watched the hatching of a brood of turkeys.

> *I concealed myself on the ground within a very few feet, and saw [the hen] raise herself half the length of her legs, look anxiously upon the eggs, cluck with a sound peculiar to the mother on such occasions, carefully remove each half-empty shell, and with her bill caress and dry the young birds, that already stood tottering and attempting to make their way out of the nest. Yes, I have seen this, and have left mother and young to better care than mine . . . to the care of their Creator and mine. I have seen them all emerge from the shell, and, in a few moments after, tumble, roll, and push each other forward, with astonishing and inscrutable instinct.*

He went on to describe a pet turkey he'd once had.

> *While at Henderson, on the Ohio, I had, among many other wild birds, a fine male Turkey, which had been reared from its earliest youth under my care, it having been caught by me when probably not more than two or three days old. It became so tame that it would follow any person who called it, and was the favourite of the little village.*

With production of both *The Birds of America* and *Ornithological Biography* in good hands, the Audubons returned to America in July 1831. It was time once again to collect more specimens and to try to get American subscriptions to his work.

During this visit, Audubon journeyed to Florida. In describing this tropical territory he wrote:

> *With what delightful feelings did we gaze on the objects around us!—the gorgeous flowers, the singular and beautiful plants, the luxuriant trees. The balmy air which we breathed filled us with animation, so pure and salubrious did it seem to be. The birds which we saw were almost all new to us; their lovely forms appeared to be arrayed in more brilliant apparel than I had ever seen before, and as they fluttered in happy playfulness among the bushes, or glided over the light green waters, we longed to form a more intimate acquaintance with them.*

While collecting specimens of pelican, cormorant, ibises, and heron, he noted with distress the destruction of the white oak groves. Huge quantities of trees were being cut down, and those that weren't perfect were left to rot. He foresaw that this destruction of habitat would be disastrous for birds and other wildlife.

Meanwhile, he had his own problems in stalking the water birds in the insect-infested muck and marsh. "If you endeavor to approach these birds in their haunts," he wrote, "they betake themselves to flight, and speed to places where they are secure from your intrusion." When the hunt was successful, however, all the tribulations were forgotten: "Seldom have I experienced greater pleasures then when on the Florida Keys, under a burning sun . . . tormented by myriads of insects [I procured] a heron new to me, and have at length succeeded in my efforts."

Returning to Boston he was joined by Lucy and both of his sons. He was elated that his family was together and he could hold up his head as a successful man. He hoped to make the continued work on his books a family business. Twenty-three-year-old Victor was sent to England in October of 1832 to see to the book while Audubon, accompanied by son John and several other assistants, headed north to the gulf of the St. Lawrence River to collect northern birds. In letters and journal entries, he described the "wonderful dreariness" of mossy rocks "heaped and thrown together as if by chance," "butterflies flitting over snow-banks," and the cold, wet fog. He made studies of gulls and gannets, guillemots and puffins. He described his first view of gannets nesting on the rocky shores, where the rocks were so thickly covered with white birds it looked like snow: "What we saw was not snow—but gannets! The whole of my party was astounded and amazed."

It was on this northern trip that his sentiments as a bird protectionist grew stronger. As a sportsman and hunter he simply enjoyed birds, as an ornithologist he was compelled to collect and study birds, and as a painter he wished to capture and mimic their beauty. Now, as a conservationist, he desired to preserve and protect these beautiful creatures.

Though he continued to shoot for food and study, he deplored the commercial killing of huge numbers of birds and the complete destruction of their eggs. He was appalled by this business of "eggers" who stripped whole islands bare of all eggs laid by birds, likening them to pirates. He noted in his journal: "This war of extermination can not last many years more. The eggers them-

selves will be the first to repent the entire disappearance of the
myriads of birds that made the coast of Labrador their summer
residence."

He also wrote: "Fur animals are scarce, and every year dimin-
ishes their numbers. . . . Where can I go now, and visit nature
undisturbed?"

The trip was successful however, and the long hours of work
paid off. He now had enough material to complete *The Birds of
America* and *Ornithological Biography*. When he returned to England he turned his attention to a second edition that would
combine the two books into one with the size of the pictures
reduced to a more normal book size.

Finally in 1839, after a period of 12 years, the original projects
were completed. *The Birds of America* included 435 plates covering
497 species of birds in four volumes. *Ornithological Biography* had
been produced in five volumes. There were probably about 175
complete copies of *The Birds* plus additional subscriptions that
were incomplete. Audubon had earned international recognition
for the book and, though he had not become rich, he had been
able to support himself and his family in some degree of comfort
from the sale of subscriptions.

He returned to the United States in the fall of 1839, and, at the
age of 54, was finally able to build a large three-story house outside
of New York City for his wife and family. He began work on a new
book, *The Viviparous Quadrupeds of North America*. For this book
he needed to see the large animals of the West so, in the spring of
1843, he traveled to St. Louis and there boarded a steamboat
owned by the American Fur Company. The steamboat headed up
the Missouri River, past Fort Leavenworth, past Council Bluffs,
arriving finally at Fort Union, a fortified trading post at the mouth
of the Yellowstone River, along the border of what is now the
states of North Dakota and Montana.

Just before reaching Fort Union he wrote:

> *June 12, Monday, 1843. We had a cloudy and showery day, and a
> high wind besides. We saw many Wild Geese and Ducks with their
> young. I saw a wolf giving chase. . . . but the finest sight of all took
> place shortly before we came to the mouth of the Yellowstone, and
> that was no less than twenty-two Mountain Rams and Ewes mixed.*

He went buffalo hunting and later related that he was nearly
trampled to death by a wounded buffalo, which was finally shot

and killed within feet of him. He was troubled by the large scale decimation of the once huge buffalo herds. In his journal he commented: "This cannot last; even now there is a perceptible difference in the size of the herds and before many years the buffalo, like the great auk, will have disappeared; surely this should not be permitted."

This would be his last wilderness adventure. Tired, and having lost his last remaining tooth, he was eager to return home. *Quadrupeds* was published in 30 numbers of five plates each between 1845 and 1848. Audubon was responsible for roughly half the figures it included, the remainder being completed largely by his son, John Woodhouse Audubon. Victor also had a hand in the work, painting many of the backgrounds.

Over the next few years his eyes began to mist over, and by 1846 he could no longer see well enough to paint. He lost interest in his books and his days consisted of long walks around his home and quiet afternoons being read to by Lucy. In January of 1851 he had a stroke, and on January 27, 1851, he died.

For several years after his death his sons continued to try to sell his work, but neither of them was ever so dedicated to it as he had been. Victor died in 1857 and John in 1862. Lucy had to sell much of what had been accumulated for living expenses, including the beautiful home she'd waited so many years to own.

━━━━━━━

But in the work that he left behind, the name of John James Audubon would live on. He wrote to Lucy once, explaining why he persevered against all odds in completing his books. "I know I am engaged in an arduous undertaking; but if I live to complete it, I will offer to my country a beautiful monument of the varied splendour of American nature, and of my devotion to American ornithology."

Judged as art, the paintings are beautiful, though some show much more care and feeling and attention to detail than others. As science too, there are some omissions and some mistakes, though these are mostly minor and understandable considering the newness of the study of birds in Audubon's day. The greatest value of his pictures is that they show living birds in their natural habitats. In the words that he wrote about them are priceless descriptions of what they ate, how they made their nests and attracted mates, the sound of their calls.

John James Audubon

Through his pictures and words he left behind a dramatic portrait of the America of his day, an America that no longer exists. The wilderness of Audubon's travels was a land of natural abundance, literally crawling with bear and deer and countless kinds of birds. Phoebes and robins and thrushes filled the trees. Passenger pigeons, now extinct, darkened the sky in flocks that numbered in the hundreds of thousands of birds. No one imagined that their numbers could ever be seriously reduced.

Although Audubon himself, as a lone hunter, was responsible for the deaths of hundreds, perhaps even thousands, of birds, we have to remember him in the context of his time, and hunting of this magnitude was commonly acceptable in his day. He himself recognized the danger in market hunting, whereby entire populations of birds would be systematically wiped out for pay. And he also foresaw that the greatest danger to the bird population would come not from the hunter so much as from loss of habitat as forests were felled and cities built.

Above all, John James Audubon had a passion for birds. Thus it was entirely appropriate that when efforts were made to protect the beautiful water birds from market hunters in the late 1800s, the name of Audubon would be invoked. In 1886, Dr. George Bird Grinnell, who had once been a student of Lucy Audubon's, first coined the term *Audubon society*. As editor of *Forest and Stream Magazine*, he invited readers to fight against the destruction of American birds. By November 1888, he had more than 48,000 members, mostly schoolchildren, in his Audubon society. Within a few years other Audubon societies had sprung up. Some of these remain independent to this day, while the majority have affiliated with the National Audubon Society, officially incorporated in 1905.

Besides the study and preservation of birdlife, the Audubon Society today gets involved in a wide array of conservation issues. Although ornithology was his niche in the wider field of naturalism, Audubon himself was concerned with much more than birds. He knew that birds need trees and wild places free from contamination in which to live. In his name, Audubon societies continue the fight to preserve the birds of America, as well as other forms of wildlife, and their habitats. When we look at Audubon's work, we can appreciate what we've already lost, and perhaps work harder to prevent further loss.

Chronology

April 26, 1785	John James Audubon is born in Saint-Domingue
1791	goes to live in France
1803	is sent to America to live at Mill Grove, Pennsylvania
1807	moves to Louisville, Kentucky with his partner, Ferdinand Rozier
April 1808	marries Lucy Bakewell
June 1809	son Victor born
November 1812	son John Woodhouse born
1819	Audubon declares bankruptcy
1820	decides to collect and paint birds for publication; travels down the Ohio and Mississippi rivers to New Orleans
April 1826	departs for England to find a publisher
November 1826	first paintings of *The Birds of America* printed
April 1831	first volume of *Ornithological Biography* published
1831–33	on a visit to America for more specimens, Audubon travels to Florida and Labrador
1839	*The Birds of America* and *Ornithological Biography* completed; Audubon returns to the United States to stay
1843	travels west to collect specimens for *The Viviparous Quadrupeds of North America*
1845–48	*Quadrupeds* published
1846	Audubon can no longer see well enough to paint
January 27, 1851	dies at home in New York at age 65

Further Reading

Works that Largely Include Audubon's Writing

The Birds of America. Foreword and descriptive captions by William Vogt (New York: MacMillan, 1962).

Audubon, by Himself. Edited by Alice Ford (Garden City, NY: The Natural History Press, 1969). A profile of Audubon from writings selected and edited by Alice Ford.

Audubon's America. The Narratives and Experiences of John James Audubon. Edited by Donald Culross Peattie (Boston, MA: Houghton Mifflin, 1940). A collection of Audubon's writings, illustrated with his drawings and paintings. Each section of Audubon excerpts is preceded by a short narrative giving background information.

Other Works

Adams, Alexander B. *John James Audubon* (New York: G. P. Putnam's Sons, 1966). Thorough biography of the life of the painter and naturalist. Over 470 pages, including short prologue and epilogue.

Durant, Mary and Michael Harwood. *On the Road with John James Audubon* (New York: Dodd, Mead & Co., 1980). The authors follow the travels of John James Audubon. Includes excerpts from Audubon's journals and published works, alternating with the authors' comments on their travels.

Lindsey, Alton A. *The Bicentennial of John James Audubon* (Bloomington, IN: Indiana University Press, 1985). Describes the life, travels, and work of Audubon. Besides chapters by Lindsey, includes essays by various scholars on related topics.

George Perkins Marsh: Enlightened Diplomat

George Perkins Marsh.
(Courtesy of Woodstock Historical Society)

*I*t must have been an odd-looking caravan that carried the U.S. minister to Turkey and his party across the Holy Lands that winter of 1851. Perched on a camel's back, George Perkins Marsh surveyed the desert land around him, land that had once been the breadbasket of Rome. His wife, Caroline, was ill and unable to walk. Rather than be left behind, she had herself strapped to a camel so that she might accompany her husband.

George Perkins Marsh

Each time the camels stopped to rest Marsh went to work on his notebooks, studiously writing down all of his observations. Everything fascinated him, from the unusual plants and animals that he saw to the depths of streams and the velocity of winds. As a boy growing up in Vermont he'd witnessed the effects of human activity on the environment around him. Here, far away in North Africa, was proof beyond all doubt that humans could dramatically and permanently change the face of nature. This information would be pondered and synthesized and would eventually make its way into a book that would insure a place among conservationists for George Perkins Marsh.

George Perkins Marsh was born in Woodstock, Vermont, on March 15, 1801. Vermont had only recently been added as a state to the United States and much of it remained a natural wilderness, but Woodstock had been settled by people of intellect and influence. George's father, Charles Marsh, was an accomplished and respected lawyer who served in the U.S. Congress while George was a young boy. He instilled in his children (George had seven brothers and sisters) a love for learning and a respect for knowledge for its own sake.

In this family, children who could demonstrate knowledge were valued. At the age of six, George was an avid reader of the family encyclopedia, though he had to read it while lying on the floor under a table because it was too heavy for him to lift. He was tutored in Latin and Greek by his older brother Charles. He studied so hard that by the time he was eight he had badly strained his eyes and nearly went blind. For several months he was forced to rest and wear a silk scarf over his eyes. Slowly he recovered his sight, but for the next several years he couldn't read at all, and for the rest of his life he would be plagued by eye strain.

Unable to read, George was forced to spend a great deal of time outdoors. With his many brothers and sisters and cousins there was no shortage of playmates. Together they ran and played and explored the wooded, hilly countryside around Woodstock. George would later recall his favorite activities of these days with fondness, "climbing high rocks, ascending Mt. Tom, losing ourselves in the woods or strolling through the meadow, never forgetting the orchard from the first formation of apples till the ripe fruit was ready for gathering."

Though young George missed his books and studying, what he gained would serve him well the rest of his life. He learned to develop his powers of observation, to obtain information by looking carefully at the world around him. He loved the many kinds of beauty to be found in nature. "The bubbling brook, the trees, the flowers, the wild animals, were to me persons, not things," he would later write.

As Marsh grew he noticed changes in the countryside around Woodstock. He noticed that more and more of the beautiful hills were becoming bare as they were stripped of their tree cover to make way for farm fields. He noticed that spring floods on the nearby Quechee River became more common as rain and snow-melt rushed into it, unslowed by the roots of trees. His father's sawmill was washed away in one such flood. Then in summer the river sometimes dried up entirely, ruining the fishing that had given the young boys such pleasure.

One day George went for a buggyride with his father. Perched between his father's knees, George recalled,

> *My father pointed out the most striking trees as we passed them, and told me how to distinguish their varieties. . . . He called my attention to the general configuration of the landscape, pointed out the direction of different ranges of the hills, told me how the water gathered on them and ran down their sides, and where the mountain streams would likely be found. . . . he stopped his horse on top of a steep hill, bade me notice how the water there flowed in different directions, and told me such a point was called a watershed. . . . I never forgot that word, or any part of my father's talk that day.*

With his eyes healed, George's "book-learning" resumed, and after a year at Phillips Academy in Andover, Massachusetts, he was sent to Dartmouth College in Hanover, New Hampshire. Classmates reported that he was so interested in his studies that he didn't take much time for friendships. When George grew tired of studying the Greek and Latin taught at the school (which he'd been studying at home since he was five), he learned French, Italian, Spanish, and Portuguese on his own. He could read classical literature in the ancient languages more easily than many people could read English.

He graduated from college in the summer of 1820. For a short while he taught at a military academy, but he was unhappy working with boys who were not eager to learn, and his own independent study was aggravating the old trouble with his eyes.

George Perkins Marsh

He returned to his family's home in Woodstock where his father and oldest brother read law to him while he rested his eyes. In 1825 he passed the bar exam and moved across the state of Vermont to Burlington to practice law.

In April 1828, Marsh married a young Burlington woman, Harriet Buell. Within a year they had a baby boy, named Charles. Then, in May 1832, George's law partner died. Soon afterward, Harriet became very ill after the birth of a second son, George Ozias. She died on August 16, 1833. Eleven days later, the older boy Charles died of complications from scarlet fever. Overcome with grief, Marsh sent baby George to Woodstock to be cared for by relatives. He buried himself in work and in studying Scandinavian languages, including Danish and Icelandic.

Gradually he began to rejoin some of the circles of friends he had made in Burlington. In 1835 he was elected to the Vermont state legislature. Though the youngest member of that body, he was well respected as one of its most intelligent.

In September 1839, he married a young schoolteacher, Caroline Crane. Caroline was 15 years younger than he, but shared many of his intellectual interests. It was to prove a match that would sustain them both through many, many years.

For the next several years Marsh tried to make a go of several business ventures, none of which could be called successful. He built a woolen mill but was forced to sell it when economic conditions made it unprofitable. The same thing happened with railroad investments, tool patenting, and marble quarrying. Though immensely intelligent, he seemed to lack a certain business sense and was often a victim of bad economic circumstances and a poor choice of business associates.

In 1843 he was elected as a Whig to serve Vermont in the U.S. Congress. Though Marsh made it a point to be physically present for almost every session of the Congress and got involved when the issues being discussed were of concern to him, when they were not, he often spent the time napping in his seat.

Marsh found much to interest him in Washington, D.C., however. He became a member of the committee that was responsible for creating the Smithsonian Institution. Not a scientist, but a man who understood the impact of science on life, Marsh found in the Smithsonian work a chance to promote his great love of knowledge.

Marsh was still struggling financially, however, and eagerly accepted the position of minister to Turkey when it was offered to him by President Zachary Taylor on May 29, 1849. He hoped that with a position in the foreign service he would be able to support himself and his family while continuing to pursue his quest for knowledge.

The Marsh party set sail from New York in September 1849. Arriving in Europe, the Marshes journeyed overland across France and Italy. Then there was a week's journey by ship across the Mediterranean to Constantinople. They finally arrived in Constantinople in late February 1850, having thoroughly enjoyed all that they'd been able to experience and observe during the nearly six months' journey.

In contrast to this, the weather and the work that awaited Marsh in Constantinople would be largely disappointing. Their living quarters were cold and expensive and the position of American ambassador was not highly respected. Marsh dealt mostly with matters of trade and refugees, and found that his meager salary was barely adequate to sustain himself and his family.

When winter approached again, Marsh decided that the best way to spend it would be on a trip to warmer climates. He eagerly set out for Egypt and the Nile River, looking forward to observing life in the desert. He was fascinated by all he saw there and was especially impressed with the camel after journeying a great distance on the back of one.

He sought to learn as much as he could from the trip, measuring everything from rainfall and temperatures to stream widths and wind velocities, collecting and preserving specimens of snakes and fish and lizards to send to the Smithsonian Institute. He observed that the mark of human presence had been left everywhere on the land. He'd already witnessed the effects of deforestation on the hillsides of the Green Mountains of Vermont. Now he viewed the desertification of once bountiful land in the Middle East. He understood the connection, realizing that these were the results of misuse of the land.

The following year he had to go to Athens to sort out a land dispute between an American citizen and the Greek government. From there he visited the Alps of Austria, comparing the forests there with those he was familiar with in Vermont. He wrote home to his brother: "The country between Graz and Gleichenberg reminds me strongly of Vermont in its natural features, but the care bestowed upon forests presents a marked contrast to our neglect of them."

As much as he knew, he always wished he knew more. He was sorry that he was unable to name every tree and plant and animal and rock he saw.

In 1853 a Democrat, Franklin Pierce, was elected to the presidency of the United States, and Marsh's appointment as minister to Turkey came to an end. Unsure of how he would support his family, he reluctantly returned to the United States. Slandered by enemies in Congress, he would spend much of the next five years trying to collect money owed him for his tenure in Constantinople.

In an effort to avoid bankruptcy, he struggled to figure out how to apply his interests and talents in a way that would earn a living. He lectured on subjects of interest to himself, but many of the listeners found his topics and delivery boring. He wrote a book on camels, encouraging their use in the American West, but sales were dismal.

He served on several commissions in Vermont, but they didn't pay much, and he made more enemies by reporting on the greed of railroad monopolies as railroad commissioner.

As fish commissioner, Marsh addressed the problem of the disappearance of fish from Vermont rivers and streams. He cited a number of causes, especially soil runoff from farming and clear-cutting of forests. He pointed out that when hills are stripped of trees, there is nothing to slow the water as it flows down the slopes in torrents, carrying topsoil and debris downhill. The resulting fast-moving high water levels were disruptive to the laying of fish eggs, and in many ways upset the fish reproduction processes. He pointed out the complexity of the relationship between fish breeding and the many factors affecting water flow in rivers. He warned that Vermont must institute environmental regulations because much more than the fishing industry was at stake.

But Vermont failed to act. In the 1870s, however, a protege of Marsh's, Spencer Baird, was able to force action at the national level. Baird gave credit to Marsh's earlier report in contributing to these early efforts at fish and soil conservation.

During the spring of 1860 Marsh began work on a book that would tie together all his observations about nature. He thought it would be "a little book" on the effects of human activity on nature. It would become much more.

But first he needed an income to sustain him while he wrote. That was supplied when Abraham Lincoln was elected president and named him minister to the newly formed kingdom of Italy.

At the age of 60, and with the United States about to be torn apart by civil war, Marsh was once again headed for Europe. He would spend the rest of his life there, working on behalf of the U.S. government, and on the book that would be the culmination of a lifetime observing nature.

All these years he'd been digesting the things he had seen and read about on his many travels. Now he would draw upon his storehouse of knowledge and the detailed journals he had kept to describe and explain the ramifications of humankind's interference in nature. He integrated what he had learned from books with what he had seen with his own eyes. He studied and analyzed the evidence, explained his conclusions, and prescribed some solutions.

During the winter of 1862–63 he worked steadily on the book he would call: *Man and Nature; or, Physical Geography as Modified by Human Action.* In a quiet villa near Pegli on the Riviera he read and thought and wrote. He found that by careful management of his schedule, he was able to devote considerable time to reading and writing and still see to his diplomatic duties. The manuscript began to take shape.

His ability to read rapidly in so many languages was a great asset in his research. With this talent he was able to access the thinking of many of the great scholars and scientists of his own era as well as of the ancient past. When completed, his bibliography and notes cited more than 200 publications on subjects ranging from astronomy to philosophy, in an amazing number of languages.

In the spring of 1863 he moved to a medieval castle south of Turin, and there he continued to work. His new home had a sunny terrace with an unobstructed view of the Alps. Whenever possible he visited the mountains, though increasing years and body weight made it more and more difficult for him to climb all the way to the glaciers he enjoyed studying.

As Marsh worked on the book, he continually found more information he wanted to include. Finally he was satisfied that he had included everything he could and he submitted it to his publisher, Scribner's, in New York City. In May 1864, it was published.

Marsh explained his purpose in the preface to the book with these words,

> . . . *to indicate the character and, approximately, the extent of the changes produced by human action in the physical conditions of the*

*globe we inhabit; to point out the dangers of imprudence and the
necessity of caution in all operations which, on a large scale, interfere
with the spontaneous arrangements of the organic or the inorganic
world; to suggest the possibility and the importance of the restoration
of disturbed harmonies and the material improvement of waste and
exhausted regions; and, incidentally, to illustrate the doctrine, that
man is, in both kind and degree, a power of a higher order than any
of the other forms of animated life, which, like him, are nourished at
the table of bounteous nature.*

Marsh opened the book with the history of the lands around the
Mediterranean Sea, one of the first areas of the planet to suffer
from the destructive effects of human civilization. This area that
had once supplied food for the Roman Empire was now a desert
wasteland because of "man's ignorant disregard of the laws of
nature." He chided that "man has too long forgotten that the earth
was given to him for usufruct alone [his use only], not for con-
sumption, still less for profligate waste." He claimed that "man is
everywhere a disturbing agent. Wherever he plants his foot, the
harmonies of nature are turned to discords." He was especially
critical of people who killed large animals for only a small part of
their body, such as the decimation of American buffalo herds for
skin and tongue.

In the second chapter he described man as a geological agent,
a fairly radical idea. By introducing foreign plants into new lands,
by hunting some animals to extinction and by sustaining and
nurturing others, humankind had created changes in the environment, often with unforeseen results. Marsh would be among the
first to point out that from the smallest insect and flower seed to
the largest mammal and tree, plants and animals each had roles
to play in the environment in which they were found, and in so
many cases, humans altered the balances that nature had established. He summed up this chapter by saying, "If man is destined
to inhabit the earth much longer, . . . he will learn to put a wiser
estimate on the works of creation."

Then he turned his attention to the role of forests. This would
be one of the longest, and most influential parts of the book.
Since his childhood buggy ride with his father through the mountainous watersheds of Vermont, the significance of trees in the
ecology had been clear to him. Trees were retainers and regulators
of moisture. They held water in the soil and held soil in place on
mountain slopes. Thoughtless deforestation contributed to

erosion and flooding and drought. He'd seen similar processes at work in southern Europe, in the Middle East, and at home in the United States.

This photo shows an area of logging near Jedediah Smith. A large portion of Marsh's book, Man and Nature, *is devoted to the subject of forests. Marsh pointed out that clear-cutting of hillside forests led to soil erosion, which damaged rivers, causing both floods and droughts, and disrupted fishing as well as commercial uses of rivers.*
(Courtesy of National Park Service, HFC Historic Collection)

George Perkins Marsh

"The destruction of the woods was man's first physical conquest, his first violation of the harmonies of inanimate nature," he wrote. He described how trees add to the fertility of soil as their fallen leaves and branches decay. He discussed in considerable detail the possible role of trees in regulating climate and precipitation, and the role of trees in relation to ground water. "With the disappearance of the forest, all is changed," he writes.

> . . . The face of the earth is no longer a sponge, but a dust heap, and the floods which the waters of the sky pour over it hurry swiftly along its slopes, carrying in suspension vast quantities of earthy particles which increase the abrading power and mechanical force of the current, and, augmented by the sand and gravel of falling banks, fill the beds of the streams, divert them into new channels and obstruct their outlets. The rivulets, wanting their former regularity of supply and deprived of the protecting shade of woods, are heated, evaporated, and thus reduced in their summer currents, but swollen to raging torrents in autumn and in spring. The channels of great rivers become unnavigable, their estuaries are choked up, and harbors are shoaled by dangerous sandbars. The earth, stripped of its vegetable glebe, grows less and less productive. Gradually it becomes altogether barren.

In places where forests have been destroyed and these consequences have not been seen, Marsh says, wait, for "the vengeance of nature for the violation of her harmonies, though slow, is sure, and the gradual deterioration of soil and climate in such exceptional regions is as certain to result from the destruction of the woods as in any natural effect to follow its cause."

In the last paragraph of this chapter he states, "We have now felled forest enough everywhere, in many districts far too much." Imagine what he'd think today.

The following chapters deal with water and sand. Besides their effects on the "life which peoples the sea," humans have gone so far as to "encroach upon the territorial jurisdiction of the ocean," with sedimentation and harbor structures. Marsh warns of the dangers of overextensive irrigation, such as the buildup of salts and the compacting of the soil. "There can be no doubt that by these operations man is exercising a powerful influence on soil, on vegetable and animal life, and on climate."

He closed with a chapter called "Projected or Possible Geographical Changes by Man," in which he further examined the effects of human manipulations of the environment, particularly in relation to joining bodies of water with canals. "These enter-prises are attended with difficulties and open to objections, which are not, at first sight, obvious. . . . There is, in many cases, an alarming uncertainty as to the effects of joining together waters which nature has put asunder."

He concludes by admonishing that we must look for unforeseen consequences of our actions, for the laws of nature "are as inflex-ible in dealing with an atom as with a continent or a planet. . . . Our inability to assign definite values to these causes of the disturbance of natural arrangements is not a reason for ignoring the existence of such causes in any general view of the relations between man and nature, and we are never justified in assuming a force to be insignificant because its measure is unknown, or even because no physical effect can now be traced to it as its origin."

When the book first appeared, the American public was dis-tracted by the Civil War, and initial sales were slow. Marsh didn't expect to earn much from it, so he gave the copyright to the United States Sanitary Commission, a Civil War charity. Fortunately for him, some more optimistic friends believed that the book would do well, and they purchased the copyright back for him for $500.

Slowly sales did improve as word got out about the fine work that Marsh had done. Reviews called the book "delightful." One called it a book "which will lure the young to observe and take delight in Nature, and the mature to respect her rights as essential to their own well-being." *The Nation* called it "one of the most useful and suggestive works ever published." Within a few months more than 1,000 copies had been sold and Scribner's prepared a second printing.

Over the following years Marsh continued to update the manu-script as he came across new research and several revised editions were published. Throughout this time scientists as well as the general public were reading and commenting on the book, and it was credited with a role in the interest in forestry that was sparked in the United States in the late 1800s. All of the important figures in American forestry, including America's first chief forester, Gifford Pinchot, noted the significance of *Man and Nature* to the movement. It was also read and quoted in Europe.

In a report requested by the U.S. commissioner of agriculture, Marsh cautioned against excessive irrigation in the arid American West and pleaded for government rather than private control of precious water resources. He cautioned that the negative effects of irrigation, the buildup of salts in the soil, the hardening of the soil, and so on, be considered before large scale irrigation projects were adopted. Later U.S. geologist John Wesley Powell would further promote these beliefs.

In Italy, court shifted from Turin to Florence, and Marsh was forced to move his household again. Later there was a move to Rome. After Lincoln was assassinated, Marsh was kept on at his post by presidents Andrew Johnson and Ulysses Grant. He served as ambassador for 21 years, a remarkable record considering that most ambassadors were recalled each time there was a change in administration. Marsh's reputation as an intellectual far exceeded his skills as a diplomat, but apparently that reputation was weighty enough that he was able to keep his job. This was fortunate for him, because he still depended on his foreign service salary to support his family in comfort.

He loved to go to the mountains of northern Italy and Switzerland in the summer. During the summer of 1882, he went to the Tuscan slopes of the Apenines. He was glad to be in the mountains again. He stayed at a hotel not far from a school of forestry, which he visited and talked with the students.

On July 23, 1882, after a pleasant day in the small village, he felt tired and went in the house to lie down. Caroline called for a doctor, but within a few hours, Marsh was dead. Two days later his body was carried down the mountainside by foresters and taken to Rome where he was buried.

In the common thinking of Marsh's day, anything people did to control nature was considered good. The extent of people's power, their ability to cause permanent damage, was relatively unexamined and unrecognized. In an age when the resources of the North American continent, if not the planet, seemed inexhaustible, Marsh was one of the first to suggest in clear and dramatic terms that the resources of the Earth were in fact exhaustible, and that much damage had already been done, some of which was irreversible. It was not just for the sake of nature, but for the sake of all humankind that action had to be taken. He hoped that by pointing these misdeeds out to people, they would mend their ways, repair the damage that had been done, and proceed in smarter behaviors.

Marsh was especially suited to see the big picture, to point out that the same processes causing destruction in North Africa

Marsh asked that everyone, including farmers, accept responsibility for the consequences of their actions on the Earth.
(Courtesy of Agricultural Research Service, USDA)

were equally destructive in Austria and in New England. While others had expressed concern about decreased waterflow in a certain river or increased soil erosion on a certain plain, Marsh took all these problems in all parts of the world and showed how they were related, how they added up to the potential for disaster on a global scale.

Marsh did not condemn farmers, or tree cutters, or livestock raisers; he'd done all these things himself. He just asked that people accept the responsibility that these activities did have effects on the land, and that where these effects were negative, care must be taken to minimize the damage. As his biographer, David Lowenthal says, "Anyone with a hoe or an axe knows what he is doing, but before Marsh, no one had seen the total effects of all axes and hoes."

He did not call for the worship of nature, simply the sensible and careful use of it. Unlike many later conservationists, he did not see humans as part of nature. More in keeping with his times, he took the view that people were superior to nature. But in stating that that superiority required wise use, he was far ahead of his day.

He wanted people to appreciate that their meddling with nature had many consequences, some of which might not be apparent at the time of the activity. Marsh said that with forethought and scientific application of knowledge, humankind could restore damaged places and prevent further destruction of others.

There is much that is presented by Marsh in *Man and Nature* that still holds true today, and its wisdom is periodically rediscovered. The new attitudes that he called for would gain in momentum, and more voices would be added to that of George Perkins Marsh. *Man and Nature* has been used again and again in the conservation movement, especially in relation to water and forests.

In 1954, nearly 100 years later, a symposium was held to discuss many of the subjects that had been approached in Marsh's book. The results of this conference were published as a book entitled *Man's Role in Changing the Face of the Earth*. The investigation continues.

Perhaps the greatest tribute to *Man and Nature* was the passing of the National Environmental Protection Act in 1969. This act requires individuals and organizations who have an impact on the environment to analyze and assess the probable effects of their actions. This was just the sort of thing Marsh had called for a century before.

"Every human action," he cautioned us, "leaves an imprint. We are never justified in assuming a force to be insignificant [just] because its measure is unknown, or even because no physical effect can be traced to it."

Chronology

March 15, 1801	George Perkins Marsh is born in Woodstock, Vermont
1820	graduates from Dartmouth College, Hanover, New Hampshire
1825	passes bar exam, opens law partnership in Burlington, Vermont
1828	marries Harriet Buell
1829	son Charles is born
1833	son George is born; Harriet and young Charles die
1835	Marsh is elected to Vermont state legislature
1839	marries Caroline Crane
1843	is elected to U.S. Congress from Vermont
1849	travels to Constantinople as U.S. ambassador to Turkey
1851	visits Egypt and the Middle East
1853	appointment as ambassador to Turkey ends; Marsh returns to the United States
1860	begins work on *Man and Nature;* receives appointment as ambassador to Italy
1864	*Man and Nature* is published
July 23, 1882	Marsh dies at age 81 while resting in an Alpine village; is buried in Rome

Further Reading

Works by George Perkins Marsh

Man and Nature. Edited by David Lowenthal (Cambridge, MA: Harvard University Press, 1965). The text in this version is the first edition of Marsh's work, published in 1864, with introduction by Lowenthal.

Other Works

Curtis, Jane and Will, and Frank Lieberman. *The World of George Perkins Marsh, America's First Environmentalist* (Woodstock, VT: Countryman Press, 1982). Biography of Marsh, suitable for young adults, illustrated with photographs.

Lowenthal, David. *George Perkins Marsh, Versatile Vermonter* (New York: Columbia University Press, 1958). More lengthy, detailed biography of Marsh. Includes photographs.

Thomas, William L. Jr., ed. *Man's Role in Changing the Face of the Earth* (Chicago, IL: The University of Chicago Press, 1956). Discusses many of the issues covered by Marsh 100 years earlier.

John Muir:
Man of the Mountains and
Wild Places

John Muir, in his later years.
(Courtesy of National Park Service, HFC Historic Collection)

*O*n March 28, 1868, the San Francisco harbor was busy, as usual, with ships both arriving and departing. One of the ships in the harbor had just arrived with passengers from New York, via the Isthmus of Panama. Two men who got off that ship walked up Market Street, noting the hubbub and clatter of business in the growing port city. One of the men stopped a carpenter busy at work to ask for the quickest way out of the city.

"But where do you want to go?" the carpenter asked.

"Anywhere that is wild," 30-year-old John Muir answered.

The carpenter directed him to a ferry that transported him across San Francisco Bay. From there he and his companion, an English adventurer named Chilwell whom he'd met on ship, hiked southward into the Santa Clara Valley and eastward toward Pacheco Pass. From there he could see the Great Central Valley, which lay below "like a lake of pure sunshine," a "vast level flower garden." Beyond were the Sierra Nevada, which he described as "the mighty Sierra, so gloriously colored and so radiant, it seemed not clothed with light, but wholly composed of it."

The two hikers crossed the San Joaquin River and Muir marveled at the wild flowers growing all around. They seemed to him more abundant than the grass. Finally they reached their goal, the Yosemite Valley. Here the Merced River wound its way through tall canyons of rock. Later he would call the Yosemite Valley "the grandest of all the . . . temples of Nature I was ever permitted to enter."

In 1864 President Abraham Lincoln had signed a proclamation setting aside Yosemite Valley and the nearby Mariposa Grove of giant redwoods for public use and recreation. Because the federal government had no system to manage what was essentially the first national park, it was turned over to the state of California, which allowed a number of commercial operations there.

After a few weeks of wandering in the mountains, living mainly on bread and tea, the two adventurers returned to civilization to find work in the fields of a local farmer. After a time the two companions parted ways. Chilwell, looking for action, was anxious to move on. But John Muir had found something in the Yosemite Valley that he was not ready to leave. He'd found health; in the cool, fresh mountain air he'd fully recovered from the malaria he'd contracted the previous year in Florida. More than that, he'd found a place he wanted to get to know better, a place he wanted to live in and study. For the rest of his days, the Yosemite Valley would be at the center of his life.

John Muir was born on April 21, 1838, in the Scottish town of Dunbar. His father, Daniel Muir, was a shopkeeper. His mother,

Ann, cared for John and his older sisters, Margaret and Sarah. While John was growing up, two more sons were born, David and Daniel Jr., and then twin girls, Mary and Annie.

Daniel Muir was extremely religious, devoting himself to the study of the Bible and the battle for salvation. When John was nearly 11, Daniel decided that America, the land of religious freedom, was the place for his family to be. Without a word of discussion, he sold his store and departed for the New World on February 19, 1849, taking John, David, and Sarah with him. The others would follow when a home was built and a farm started.

After landing in New York, Daniel led his three children over land and river and lake to Milwaukee, Wisconsin. From there they journeyed by horse and wagon to Marquette County, finally choosing an 80-acre plot near the Fox River a few miles from Portage to call their own. Fountain Lake Farm, as Daniel Muir named the property, came complete with trees and bird nests, bogs, and meadows. "Oh, that glorious Wisconsin wilderness," John would later say of it. "I was set down in the midst of pure wildness where every object excited endless admiration and wonder." He was now experiencing first hand the natural wonders of America that John James Audubon had described and that he had heard about in Scotland. He would spend as much time as he could exploring every inch of the farm, though soon the hard work of clearing and plowing the land and building a proper house would leave little time for play. Just before winter mother and the rest of the children rejoined the family. One more baby, Joanna, was born a few years later.

Daniel Muir believed that souls were saved by physical toil and lost not an opportunity to remind his children of this. John was forced to work harder and harder as his father continued to buy more land for the farm.

In what little spare time he had, John liked to tinker and whittle, creating inventions purely from his head. One of his inventions he called "an early rising machine." This machine was a sort of alarm clock that would tip a bed up at an appointed hour. During the summer of 1860, a neighbor convinced him to show his inventions at the state fair in Madison. This was just the push out of the nest that he needed.

John and his machines were a great sensation at the fair, but what interested John most was the nearby University of Wisconsin. He went to see the dean about the possibility of attending classes. He found that even a poor farm boy like himself, with little formal education and practically no money, could attend college classes if he worked hard, and hard work was something he was used to. He was especially excited about studying the science of botany, since he'd already spent years collecting and studying leaf and flower specimens at home. Scattered around his room in Madison, over and around his machines, were many jars of various shapes and sizes with bits of flowers and plants to study.

When the Civil War erupted in 1861, Muir was disturbed to see light-hearted boys set off to war, only to return broken and ill. He considered studying to become a doctor to alleviate some of the pain.

But other things were calling him. He was so enthralled by the field lectures on geology given by the university's Dr. Ezra Carr that he would later say, "I shall not forget the Doctor who laid before me the great book of Nature." Professor Carr's wife Jeanne befriended Muir, and throughout his travels in later years, the two would write long and encouraging letters to each other.

In March of 1864, shortly before his 26th birthday, Muir exchanged the University of Wisconsin for the "University of the Wilderness," as he called it, setting out for Canada to collect botanical specimens and probably to avoid the Civil War draft as well.

One day while wandering in a swamp in Ontario he found a beautiful and rare orchid. It very much pleased him to find such beauty in a place where it seemed to serve no practical purpose; it just was. He wrote of this experience years later, saying, "I sat down beside it and fairly cried for joy."

He supported himself by working in sawmills and factories, returning to the United States in the spring of 1866. He then went to work in a carriage-parts factory in Indianapolis. One evening in March 1867, Muir was working late in the factory, adjusting a machine belt. Suddenly the sharp file he was using slipped from his hand and flew up into his eye. As he gazed out a window in horror, the sight gradually dimmed and went out completely in the right eye. Within a few days he also lost sight in the left eye as well, as that eye responded to the injury to the other.

At first he feared that he would be blinded forever until he was examined by a specialist who reported that when the damaged eye refilled with fluid, he would see again. For a month he waited impatiently in a darkened room, being read to, and telling stories.

When his sight returned, his former employers offered him an increase in salary and shorter hours to return to the factory, but he declined. The fear that by his work on man's creations he could lose forever the gift of seeing God's creations had helped hir know where he belonged. After a visit home to see his family, and a short train ride, he departed from Louisville, Kentucky on foot, planning to walk roughly a thousand miles to the Gulf of Mexico, and from there sail to South America. He carried a journal in which he'd written "John Muir, Earth-Planet, Universe."

As he tramped through Kentucky, Tennessee, and Georgia, he witnessed the misery of people broken by war. Everywhere were deserted farms and homes, and desperate hungry men roamed the countryside. But Muir took comfort in the beauty of plants and in the friendship of good people it was his luck to meet.

By the time he reached the gulf coast of Florida, he was severely ill with malaria. Near death, he was cared for by a kind local family. While recovering he wrote in his journal some of his thoughts regarding people's place in nature. Disagreeing with those who felt that all of nature was created for the pleasure of humankind, Muir wrote,

> *Nature's object in making animals and plants might possibly be first of all the happiness of each one of them, not the creation of all for the happiness of one. Why ought man to value himself as more than an infinitely small composing unit of the one great unit of creation?. . . The universe would be incomplete without man; but it would also be incomplete without the smallest transmicroscopic creature that dwells beyond our conceitful eyes and knowledge.*

When Muir was feeling better he sailed to Cuba, but he continued to suffer recurring bouts of fever. Deciding that cool moutain air was the proper remedy, he sailed first to New York, where he was able to board a ship for San Francisco (via the Isthmus of Panama), arriving in California on March 28, 1868.

After his first brief visit to Yosemite Valley, Muir worked a number of odd jobs, saving money to return for a longer look. During the winter (1868–69) he worked as a shepherd. Though he despised the stupid, timid sheep, he was happy to have a job that allowed him to spend most of his time outdoors, thinking, sketching, and writing down his thoughts.

When summer came and the sheep headed for higher places in ˹e Sierra, Muir headed that way too. He hated what the sheep ᵗhe lush grasses and flowers of the mountain meadows, ᷈ "hooved locusts." But he was soon caught up in the ₙess of the high Sierra. He would later recount his ˻ book entitled *My First Summer in the Sierra.*

John Muir

In July 1869, he reached a place where he could look down on Yosemite Valley from high in the mountains. Wanting a better look, he crawled right to the edge of a cliff, and would later say,

John Muir first visited the breathtaking falls of Yosemite in 1868,
when he was 30 years old.
(Courtesy of National Park Service, HFC Historic Collection)

"I could not help fearing a little that the rock might split off and let me down, and what a down!—more than three thousand feet." But an inner force seemed to take over and gave him the confidence and agility to continue forward. He took off his shoes and stockings and shuffled carefully along a narrow ledge, only about three inches wide, just above the spot where Yosemite Creek plunged over the wall of rock in the spectacular Yosemite Falls.

This and other adventures he had while exploring during this time made Muir extremely happy. "No pain here, no dull empty hours, no fear of the past, no fear of the future," he wrote. "I gaze and sketch and bask."

In November he got a job working for the owner of the Hutchings Hotel in Yosemite Valley. He was employed to work in the sawmill; a great deal of lumber was needed for repairs and expansions to the hotel and other buildings in the valley. Muir took the job with the understanding that he would cut no live trees for the mill. There were plenty of pines downed by the ravages of weather to keep the mill busy, and he would work only on those.

He built himself a sturdy little cabin of rough pine with a floor of flat stones carried from Yosemite Creek. A stream passed through a corner of the cabin, "with just current enough to allow it to sing and warble in low, sweet tones." He slept in a hammock with a view through his window of Yosemite Falls.

Along with his work in the sawmill and carpentry chores, Muir was expected to help guide some of the tourists who were in those days just beginning to discover the wonders of Yosemite.

He had little patience for timid ladies from Boston in high-heeled shoes who squealed in fright at the sight of a small snake and who could merely comment "how pretty" at the sight of the great falls. But his dear friend Jeanne Carr, now with her husband at the University of California in Oakland, sent travelers to him who shared a deeper respect and appreciation of nature.

From time to time Carr tried to coax Muir out of the wilderness, worried about the life of solitude that he led. But though he too worried that everyone else in his family had settled down, he felt sure that this life in the wilderness was right for him. He confided to his journal: "I will follow my instincts, be myself for good or ill, and see what will be the upshot. As long as I live, I'll hear waterfalls and birds and winds sing."

As Muir studied the valley and the peaks that rose from it, he became more and more convinced that it had been formed by the slow, grinding movement of ancient glaciers. He wrote in his journal that "this entire region must have been overswept by ice." This was in contrast to the more popular theory of the geologist Josiah Whitney, who claimed that the valley had been formed by the lowering of the ground in an earthquake.

On hearing of Muir's theory, Whitney called him "only a sheep-herder" and an "ignoramus." But Muir continued to investigate in the mountains themselves and became more and more sure of his theory. Eventually his dedicated sleuthing in the recesses of the mountains paid off. He discovered in an untraveled wilderness area of the Sierra a glacial moraine (an area of rock and silt left by a glacier) and an actual small but "living" glacier.

In May 1871, he met Ralph Waldo Emerson when the 68-year-old writer and philosopher visited Yosemite Valley. Muir tried to talk him into spending a night in the mountains under the stars with him, but Emerson's friends intervened, fearing for the old man's health. This was something Muir could never understand, for to him, the only healthy place to be was in the mountains, under the stars.

In the fall of 1871, he decided to try shaping his thoughts about the formation of Yosemite into an article. He was self-conscious and hesitant, but the support of people who'd come to believe in his theory finally convinced him to try. In an article entitled "Yosemite Glaciers" he wrote, "I have been drifting about among the rocks of this region for several years, anxious to spell out some of the mountain truths which are written here." He submitted it to the New York *Tribune,* which accepted and published and even paid for the article in December 1871, to Muir's surprise and delight. In 1872 he sold another article to the *Tribune,* and several articles to *Overland Monthly,* a popular West Coast magazine. These articles were well received and provided Muir with some much-appreciated income that allowed him to continue his wilderness life.

There were now a number of people who encouraged Muir to "come East" and teach at Harvard or some other institution. But Muir had no desire to sit in a building in a city and teach. He wanted to live his studies in the vastness of nature. He knew that he had been "too long wild," as he put it, to fit into the prim and proper world of a New England university.

He did however enjoy the company of people who shared his interests. Now he found that there were a number of these in the San Francisco/Oakland area. Among these were the artist William Kieth, the geologist Joseph LeConte, the educator John Swett, and, of course, the Carrs. He arranged to spend winters in the homes of these friends where he could write and converse and then return in the summers to tramp in the wilderness, gathering his thoughts and regaining peace.

He searched his notebooks for ideas on things to write about. In his writing he stayed close to the emotions of his experiences. In one piece he described a rainstorm on Mount Shasta.

John Muir in the Hetch Hetchy Valley of Yosemite National Park,
one of several areas he worked to have set aside as places where people
could "look at nature's loveliness."
(Courtesy of National Park Service, HFC Historic Collection)

John Muir

A vigorous thunderbolt crashes through the crisp sunny air, ringing like steel on steel, its startling detonation breaking into a spray of echoes among the rocky canyon below. Then down comes a cataract of rain to wild gardens and groves. The big crystal drops tingle the pine needles, plash and splatter on granite pavements, and pour adown the sides of ridges . . . in a net-work of gray bubbling rills.

These were vivid descriptions of the natural world such as Henry David Thoreau had written, but even wilder considering the rugged wilderness of the Sierra as compared to the peaceful quiet of a New England woods. He combined descriptions with adventures as Audubon had done. One of his most popular pieces was his description of another storm in which he climbed to the top of a tall Douglas fir and, with his coat whipping and the tree thrashing, listened to the sound of the wind. He described himself as participating in adventures with nature, learning from nature, never as a man out to conquer nature.

In a letter to Jeanne Carr he once wrote: "I care to live only to entice people to look at nature's loveliness." He was glad that people enjoyed his writing, but he really wanted them to see nature for themselves, saying, "One day's exposure to mountains is better than cartloads of books."

Back and forth he would go, from mountain wilderness to the city firesides of friends, for he needed both. He needed the spiritual release he found in the mountains, but he also needed the social comradeship he found among his many friends in the San Francisco/Oakland area.

During a trip into the Sierras in the fall of 1875, he watched in horror as giant sequoias were thoughtlessly cut down. It saddened and angered him to see the wild places destroyed by loggers, miners, and ranchers. He began to think more about the dangers of land and resource monopoly that led to such abuse.

In February 1876, a Sacramento newspaper published an article of his entitled: "God's First Temples—How Shall We Preserve Our Forests." In it he called for laws to protect the wilderness. This was the beginning of his use of his pen for the work of preservation. "Everybody needs beauty as well as bread," he wrote, "places to play in and pray in, where Nature may heal and cheer and give strength to body and soul alike."

By the spring of 1878 he was finding reasons to visit the home of the Strentzel family, to whom he'd been introduced by Jeanne Carr. Dr. Strentzel, a Polish-born physician, and his wife and

31-year-old daughter, Louie Wanda, operated a prosperous fruit farm near Martinez, not far from Oakland. Though he still loved to wander, Muir was also drawn to family companionship and gradually he began courting Louie Wanda.

This did not deter him from wandering, however. In the summer of 1879 he visited the Olympic Mountains of Oregon and British Columbia, and then went on to Alaska.

Guided by several Native Americans, Muir and a friend paddled through islands and icebergs to Glacier Bay. He walked a little ways across a glacier that would later be named for him. (He was the first white man known to see what is now Glacier Bay National Monument.)

Freezing weather forced him to return to civilization and to the Strentzel ranch, where he and Louie were married on April 14, 1880. There he worked in the orchards from April to July. Harvest would not begin until October, so his wife agreed that he could have until then to return to the wilderness. He was anxious to return to the glaciers of the North.

At Fort Wrangell, on Alaska's southern coast, he was reunited with his friend of the year before, S. Hall Young. This time, besides several Indian guides as before, Young's small black dog Stickeen accompanied the group. Muir would later write a book about this dog and the adventure they shared on a glacier.

Returning to Louie in October, Muir settled into life on the ranch, working in the fields, bringing fruit to the market, carrying laundry bags full of money to the bank. On March 25, 1881, the Muirs' first daughter, Annie Wanda, was born. Muir was immensely proud of the baby and loved to carry her around the ranch. He wanted his daughter to "go to nature's school," so, as she grew, he taught her the names of flowers and birds and encouraged her to draw pictures of the beautiful things of nature, even in his personal journals.

But his health was suffering from life as a farmer. He had grown exceedingly thin and developed a hacking cough. When an opportunity to accompany an Arctic expedition presented itself, he was easily talked into going. He was able to collect some rare botanical specimens and to discuss his favorite topics, glaciers and conservation, with other learned men on the trip.

On January 23, 1886, a second daughter, Helen, was born. She was sickly at first, and care and concern for her added to the burdens Muir carried. He spent many long hours nursing the child

Tuolumne Meadows, in the northeastern portion of Yosemite National Park,
provide some of the spectacular scenery that prompted Muir to write,
"Everybody needs beauty as well as bread."
(Courtesy of National Park Service, HFC Historic Collection)

and attending to the orchards. Finally, he could stand it no more; he needed to get back into the wilderness.

And the wilderness needed him too. As he ventured back into the mountains, he was appalled to see how much damage had been done during his years away. The mountainsides were being stripped of trees. It bothered him that he had been home earning money and had not been here in the wilderness to protect it, or at least to protest.

In August 1888, he climbed Mount Rainier. Here he regained strength, health, and sense of purpose. Meanwhile, Louie realized that owning the orchard was draining her husband and taking him away from the great work he needed to do. "A ranch that needs and takes the sacrifice of a noble life, or work, ought to be flung away," she wrote him. Over the next few years she saw to it that much of the land was sold or leased so that once again John Muir would be free to roam the mountains and share their beauty with others through his writing.

In June 1889, Muir met Robert Underwood Johnson, editor of an influential magazine called the *Century*. The two journeyed together to the Yosemite Valley, noting the damage being done by men and sheep. Muir was moved to tears and Johnson challenged him to use his pen to do something about it. Johnson would carry the fight back East by publishing Muir's battle cry in the *Century*.

So Muir wrote of the damage to the valley that occurred under state control, asking that the mountains surrounding the valley be made into a national park, as had been done for Yellowstone by a vote of Congress in 1872.

When "Treasures of the Yosemite" was published in August 1890, and "Features of the Proposed National Park" the following month, the public interest in Yosemite was sparked. Editorials around the country agreed with Muir and Johnson that Yosemite should become a national park. Congressmen were besieged with letters. John W. Noble, secretary of the interior, and William Henry Harrison, president of the United States, were in favor and worked for passage of the bill. On September 25, 1890, Sequoia National Park was created. A few days later General Grant National Park (which would later become part of Kings Canyon National Park) was created. October 1, 1890, the Yosemite National Park bill was passed, with boundaries nearly identical to those proposed by Muir. (At this time the Yosemite Valley and the Mariposa Grove were still under the control of the state of California.)

To restore himself from the fight, Muir headed for Alaska and Muir Glacier. While doctors reminded him that he was 52 years old and urged him to rest in bed, he decided that the wilderness was what he needed. Sleeping on his sled, alone, on a glacier, frozenness all around, listening to the howling of wolves, and exhilarated by the wonderfulness of the chance, he pitied all others who never had such an opportunity. What many people would have considered flirting with death, he considered truly living. Once when someone had offered him sympathy for being caught in a storm, Muir had replied, "Don't pity me. Pity yourselves. You stay at home, dry and defrauded of all the glory I have seen. Your souls starve in the midst of abundance!"

Muir's next move on behalf of conservation was to organize a group that would work to preserve California's natural heritage.

John Muir

On May 28, 1892, Muir and a group of concerned individuals met in the office of Attorney Warren Olney and launched the Sierra Club. Its purpose was to "explore, enjoy, and render accessible the mountain regions of the Pacific Coast; to publish authentic information concerning them; to enlist the support and cooperation of the people and government in preserving the forests and other natural features of the Sierra Nevada Mountains." Muir became the club's first president and would serve in that post until his death.

In 1892 lumbermen and cattle and sheep ranchers organized Congressional favor for a bill to reduce the size of Yosemite National Park, being particularly concerned with certain lush forest areas. The bill passed in the House, but then Muir and the Sierra Club jumped into the fight. By giving interviews to newspapers and sending telegrams to Senators, Muir helped to get the bill tabled in the Senate. The vigilance of the Sierra Club helped protect the Yosemite this time, and the battle proved that the need for such an organization was very real.

After a trip to Europe in which he visited his Scottish birthplace, he set to work revising a series of essays about the Sierras to put in book form. *The Mountains of California,* published in 1894, became his first book. Its first print run sold out in a few months, and it would continue to sell through many more printings. It aroused many people to get involved in the movement to preserve the nation's dwindling forests. It also provoked lumbermen to see the need to organize opposition to the forest preservation movement.

In July 1896, Muir joined the Forestry Commission, a group of scientists examining the condition of the nation's forests. The commission included Gifford Pinchot, one of the nation's first trained foresters. Everywhere they saw the damage inflicted by lumbermen, miners, railroads, and livestock. From the Black Hills of South Dakota to the Bitter Root Mountains of Montana to the Cascades of Washington and Oregon, the story was the same. Whole mountain slopes had been stripped of the trees that played such an important role in the water supply of the watershed areas.

In February 1897, retiring president Grover Cleveland was given the commission's report. It recommended (among other things) that 13 "forest reserves" be set aside. They recommended that these reserves be preserved as wilderness areas, closed to grazing and other commercial uses. As one of his last acts as president, Cleveland set aside some 21 million acres of forest land. Western senators in the control of lumber, mining, ranching, and railroad interests screamed for impeachment. Muir was called upon to explain the "preservationist" cause to the public.

The August 1897 issue of the *Atlantic Monthly* carried an article by Muir entitled "The American Forests." It was one of his greatest appeals on behalf of the wilderness. He described the "slaughter" of trees, saying,

> *Any fool can destroy trees. They cannot run away; and if they could, they would still be destroyed—chased and hunted down as long as fun or a dollar could be got out of their bark and hides. . . . It took more than three thousand years to make some of the trees in these western woods—trees that are still standing in perfect strength and beauty, waving and singing in the mighty forests of the Sierra. Through all the wonderful, eventful centuries since Christ's time— and long before that—God has cared for these trees, saved them from drought, disease, avalanches, and a thousand straining, leveling tempests and floods; but He cannot save them from fools—only Uncle Sam can do that.*

When mining and grazing and lumbering interests protested that America needed the resources being "locked up" in the national parks and forest reserves, Muir called them "patriotic thieves," pretending to be interested in the national good when they were really motivated only by greed.

Later that month as Muir was returning from a trip to Alaska he stopped in a Seattle hotel. He saw that Gifford Pinchot happened to be there as well. Pinchot was quoted in the paper as saying that sheep caused no harm to the forest. Muir knew otherwise, and he knew that Pinchot also knew otherwise. He was furious. He confronted the forester with his quote. Pinchot said that yes, he had said that. Muir then said that he would have nothing to do with Pinchot again.

Pinchot believed that the single-most important reason to conserve forests was to "ensure a steady supply of timber for human prosperity." The fact that trees might be beautiful to look at or forests home to wildlife was only secondarily important to him. He believed in regulated use of forests.

In an article entitled "Wild Parks and Forest Reservations of the West," published in January 1898 in the *Atlantic,* Muir attacked the "utilitarian" focus of Pinchot's conservationism in favor of his own more aesthetic, spiritual, appreciative focus of conservation. The gap between the philosophies of the two influential conservationists was widening.

John Muir

In 1901 Muir's book *Our National Parks* was published. In it he wrote: "Walk quietly in any direction and taste the freedom of the mountaineer. . . . Climb the mountains and get their good tidings. Nature's peace will flow into you as sunshine flows into trees. The winds will blow their own freshness into you, and the storms their energy, while cares will drop off like autumn leaves."

Muir believed in the power of getting people into the wilderness. "Few are altogether deaf to the preaching of pine trees," he told a Sierra Club gathering in 1895. "Their sermons on the mountains go to our hearts; and if people in general could be got into the woods, even for once, to hear the trees speak for themselves, all difficulties in the way of forest preservation would vanish."

As more people visited the national parks and forest reserves that he had done so much to help create, Muir wrote: "Thousands of tired, nerve-shaken, over-civilized people are beginning to find out that going to the mountains is going home; that wildness is a necessity; and that mountain parks and reservations are useful not only as fountains of timber and irrigating rivers, but as fountains of life." He believed that by coming to the wilderness everyone could achieve a good relationship with nature.

In May 1903, he took the president, Theodore Roosevelt, camping in Yosemite. The two spent a night under the stars on a bed of pine boughs. Muir talked until late in the night, filling the president with his passionate belief in the need to save the trees. He made the president see that the answer to California's water supply problem lay in the careful preservation of mountain forests. Most of all he talked about the mismanagement of Yosemite Valley in the hands of the state of California. He proposed that it be turned back over, or receded, to the federal government to be included in the national park. While they slept it snowed and in the morning they woke covered with several inches of snow, which Roosevelt found delightful.

Then Muir took a year off for a world trip. Worn out by visits to museums and art galleries, he was revived by the ancient wondrous forests of Russia. One of his favorite stops was the simple lunch of brown bread, boiled eggs, wild berries, and tea he enjoyed in a Finnish peasant cabin. He saw the Himalayas of India and the Pyramids of Egypt. He classified plants in Australia.

Returning in the spring of 1904, he rejoined the battle for the recession of Yosemite Valley, a fight that his Sierra Club had continued to wage while he was gone.

Many leaders in the national government were in favor of the proposal, but it would require the approval of the state legislature as well. Muir and many others worked hard to convince the California State Legislature to pass the bill to recede. Muir detested politics but understood the need, and the bill passed in California. Then they had to fight to get the grant accepted by the national Congress. Finally, in June 1906, the valley became part of the Yosemite National Park.

Meanwhile Muir's daughter Helen was sick with pneumonia. Doctors prescribed desert air, so he took her and her sister Wanda to Arizona in May 1905. In June John and daughter Wanda rushed home because Louie was very ill. She died on August 6. After the funeral John and Wanda returned to Arizona to be with Helen. To quench his grief, John spent time in the desert of Arizona, being with nature. He started the work that would lead to the protection of Arizona's Petrified Forest, first as a national monument. Later it would become a national park. He also promoted a national park in the Grand Canyon.

As he worked for the creation of new parks, trouble arose in the park he'd already worked so hard for. It seemed that the city of San Francisco needed water, and certain officials had become convinced that a reservoir in the Hetch Hetchy Valley, in the northwest corner of Yosemite Park, was the only answer. Despite its rather unattractive name, Hetch Hetchy was a valley every bit as beautiful as Yosemite, beauty that would be lost forever if a dam were built there. Those who supported the dam felt that the water needs of San Francisco outweighed the value of the valley. Angrily Muir denounced the plan. "Dam Hetch Hetchy!" he wrote. "As well dam for water tanks the people's cathedrals and churches, for no holier temple has ever been consecrated by the heart of man."

Through the first decade of the 20th century Muir gave his best to the battle. He wrote letters and newspaper articles, he sent telegrams when letters wouldn't do. He published books that were magnificent testimonials to the value of undeveloped wilderness. (In 1911, *My First Summer in the Sierra* and in 1912, *The Yosemite* were published. In 1913, *The Story of My Boyhood and Youth* appeared.) In 1911 he finally visited the Amazon River, where he had been headed before first coming to Yosemite all those years before.

But the battle for Hetch Hetchy was lost when a bill authorizing construction of a dam in the valley was passed in December 1913. The defeat left Muir exhausted and disheartened that preservationism had been so mercilessly defeated by commercialism.

He marshaled his energies to work on a book about his adventurous journeys to Alaska. With his health fading, he went to visit his daughter Helen in Southern California. Almost immediately he became sick with pneumonia and was taken to the hospital in Los Angeles where he died on December 24, 1914.

Muir's unfinished manuscript for *Travels in Alaska* was by his bedside when he died. It was typed and edited and published in 1915. Many collections of his letters and journals have also been published since his death.

Though saddened by the defeat over Hetch Hetchy, Muir did not despair for the future, saying that "the battle for conservation will go on endlessly. It is part of the universal warfare between right and wrong." As author Michael P. Cohen would later write: "Many of the issues Muir explored are eternal and have no final answers. Perhaps what he had to teach was that a man might never solve all the problems he began to uncover when he asked 'What is the right relationship between Man and Nature, Civilization and Wilderness?'"

There were many young men and women, both within the Sierra Club and without, ready to carry on the work he had started, inspired by his words and deeds. Some were working to establish a national park service to look after the growing number of national parks. On August 25, 1916, the National Park Service was created with Stephen T. Mather as the first director. Its creation was at least partially due to the resolve of conservationists to keep such acts as the damming of Hetch Hetchy from happening again.

For having a hand in the creation of so many of our national parks, Muir is sometimes known as "the father of the national parks." Since his death millions of people have taken his advice to "climb the mountains and get their good tidings." More than three million each year visit his beloved Yosemite National Park. And in California, each April 21, John Muir's birthday, the day before Earth Day, is proclaimed John Muir Day.

Chronology

April 21, 1838	John Muir is born in Dunbar, Scotland
1849	emigrates to America; family settles on a farm in Wisconsin
1860	Muir enrolls at University of Wisconsin
1867	temporarily loses sight in a factory accident; departs for 1,000-mile walk to Florida
1868	arrives in San Francisco; hikes into Yosemite Valley
1871	meets R. W. Emerson; "Yosemite Glaciers" published in New York *Tribune*
1879	Muir first visits Alaska; walks on what will be named Muir Glacier
April 14, 1880	marries Louie Strentzel
September 1880	returns to Alaska; experiences perilous adventure with dog, later published as *Stickeen*
1888	Louie sells much of the orchard to allow Muir to travel and write
1890	Yosemite National Park created
1892	Muir founds Sierra Club
1894	first book, *Mountains of California,* published
May 1903	Muir camps in Yosemite with Theodore Roosevelt
June 1906	Yosemite Valley becomes part of Yosemite National Park
December 1913	battle to stop the damming of Hetch Hetchy is lost
December 24, 1914	Muir dies of pneumonia in a Los Angeles hospital

Further Reading

Works by John Muir

Stickeen (Boston, MA: Houghton Mifflin, 1909). The story of Muir's adventures with the dog Stickeen on a glacier in Alaska.

My First Summer in the Sierra (Boston, MA: Houghton Mifflin, 1911). Muir describes the summer he first arrived in California, beginning with sheep herding in June 1889, through his first visit to the Yosemite Valley in September 1889.

The Story of My Boyhood and Youth (Boston, MA: Houghton Mifflin, 1913). Muir's own story of his boyhood in Scotland and his growing up in Wisconsin.

Travels in Alaska (Boston, MA: Houghton Mifflin, 1915). Describes his five visits to Alaska.

Other Works

Brower, Kenneth. *Yosemite. An American Treasure* (Washington, DC: National Geographic Society, 1990). Describes the beauty and history of the national park.

Fox, Stephen. *John Muir and His Legacy. The American Conservation Movement* (Boston: Little, Brown & Co., 1981). Both a biography of Muir and a history of conservation from Muir's day to 1980. Includes information on Aldo Leopold, Olaus Murie, Rachel Carson, and David Brower.

Silverberg, Robert. *John Muir, Prophet Among the Glaciers* (New York: G. P. Putnam's Sons, 1972). Interesting and readable biography for young adults.

Wadsworth, Ginger. *John Muir, Wilderness Protector* (Minneapolis: Lerner Publications, 1992). Biography for schoolchildren.

Wolfe, Linne Marsh. *Son of the Wilderness. The Life of John Muir* (New York: Alfred A. Knopf, 1945). One of the earliest comprehensive biographies of Muir. Wolfe worked with Muir's daughters in writing this biography.

Aldo Leopold: Father of Wildlife Management, Protector of Wilderness, Philosopher of the Land Ethic

Aldo Leopold.
(Courtesy of the Aldo Leopold Shack Foundation)

*O*n a January day in 1935, a middle-aged man drove up a rutted country road in Sauk County, Wisconsin. When he found the place he was looking for, he stopped his car and got out. This was the worn-out, abandoned farm to which he'd been given directions.

Aldo Leopold

There was no farmhouse; it had long since burned down and only the crumbling remains of the cellar showed where it had been. The only structure still standing was an old chicken coop. With the cold wind blowing from the nearby Wisconsin River, the landscape must have looked as desolate as the economy of the nation in this depression year. But to Aldo Leopold, it looked just right. He'd been looking for a place to begin putting some of his theories of land use into practice; what better spot than this poor abandoned farm. He knew that this wind-swept expanse of weeds and brush had once supported a healthy variety of plant and animal life, before it had been turned to cornfields and then deserted when the soil wore out. He wanted to see it restored to its bountiful prairie condition.

———

Aldo Leopold was born January 11, 1887. His family's home was on the bluffs overlooking the Mississippi River as it flowed past Burlington, Iowa. Together with his brothers Carl and Frederick and sister Marie, Aldo enjoyed hours of outdoor recreation in the countryside around their home. Often this included hunting excursions with their father, who passed on a sense of responsible sportsmanship to his children. For example, before the children were allowed to carry a gun, they had to tote a rifle-sized stick for awhile and demonstrate that they could be as careful with it as they would have to be with a gun.

As he grew older, Mr. Leopold began leaving his own gun behind, but he continued to take outings in the woods with the children, pointing out such sights as a muskrat house and the life inside a decayed log. Though Aldo would remain an enthusiastic sportsman throughout his life, he credited his father with encouraging him to be as interested in following animals with binoculars and notepad as with gun.

Living near the Mississippi River, young Aldo was able to witness the yearly migrations of many species of beautiful and interesting birds. When he was 11 years old, he wrote in a journal: "I like to study birds. I like the wren best of all birds. We had thirteen nests of wrens in our yard last summer"—and he went on to list the 39 species of birds found around his home.

After completing high school in Burlington, Aldo continued his education in the East, first at Lawrenceville Preparatory School in New Jersey, then at Yale University in Connecticut.

Lawrenceville was located in a rural setting that suited Leopold just fine. He continued to spend as much time as possible outside, just as he had as a boy. He wrote long, detailed letters to his parents, describing what he called his "tramps."

For example, he once wrote to them of a chance meeting with a particularly beautiful bird, speaking of himself in second person. "Perfectly motionless, a bird with spread tail and greenish back perches on the trunk of a sapling. He turns! A flash of black and gold! And Ye Gods!—A Hooded Warbler! . . . Nervously you fumble for glasses, get them focused . . . and look and look and look."

Never content just to walk, Leopold walked with his eyes wide open, his mind seeking answers to questions. He wondered why he saw so many phoebes gathered where wild skunk cabbage grew. He reasoned that perhaps this foul-smelling plant attracted many insects, which in turn attracted birds. Many hours of observation and investigation followed until he found his theory to be true. He took great satisfaction in solving these natural mysteries.

In September 1905, he arrived in New Haven, Connecticut, to begin his studies in science and forestry. Under the leadership of Gifford Pinchot, Yale was preparing America's first foresters to work in the newly created national forests. Here Leopold received the book-learning to combine with his love of hunting and nature. He graduated in 1909. Now, armed with a master's degree in forestry and a love for the natural world, he was ready to put his interests to work for the U. S. Forest Service.

His first assignment was in the Apache National Forest, in what was then Arizona Territory, only 20-some years since Geronimo and his Apache warriors had surrendered, four and a half centuries after the explorations of the Spanish explorer Coronado. Leopold's responsibilities included supervising workers whose job it was to report on the amount of potential lumber in the forest, and to recommend the best routes for new logging roads.

Leopold loved being in the forest, though he was more interested in studying the trees as permanent residents of the land than as a crop to be harvested. He enjoyed riding horseback across the range, becoming increasingly disturbed by the abuse of land that he detected.

He was also concerned about the status of wildlife, especially such game animals as deer and elk. Much of the wildlife that remained in the Southwest sought refuge in the national forests, and Leopold supported the Forest Service's program to restore such wildlife to greater numbers. One of the methods of increasing the number of game animals was decreasing the number of predators, such as wolves and coyotes, bears and mountain lions. Though Leopold supported this program, he was still moved by watching "a fierce green fire" die from the eyes of an old wolf he and a party of foresters had shot. He would write of this folly in a beautiful essay years later when he came to realize that the wolf and other predators had a role to play in the ecosystem of the wilderness.

From the Apache he was sent to the Carson National Forest near Santa Fe, New Mexico, where he was promoted to the rank of forest supervisor in March 1912. Here he met and courted Estella Bergere, daughter of a well-respected Santa Fe family. They were married on October 9, 1912.

Much of the land of the Carson National Forest was heavily grazed by cattle and sheep. Leopold became acquainted on a first-hand basis with such problems as erosion of hillsides, depletion of forage grasses that leads to takeover by other plants, and the decrease in wildlife that result from over-grazing.

Leopold's work often required extended horseback trips across the range in all kinds of weather. On one such trip, in April of 1913, he slept out in both rain and snow, alternately being soaked and frozen, over a period of several days. First his knees and then his arms began to swell, and he thought he had rheumatism. By the time he reached medical help in Santa Fe, his whole body was inflamed and swollen, and he was near death with acute nephritis (kidney failure). He was sent to bed and told to avoid overexertion at all costs, as any recurrence could well be fatal.

As the months of recuperation dragged on, Leopold did a lot of reading. One book that would have a tremendous influence on him was *Our Vanishing Wild Life,* by William Temple Hornaday. In this book Hornaday, spearhead of the wildlife protection movement and ardent opponent of sport hunting, presented strong arguments for the preservation of threatened game species. From this point on Leopold's interest in the conditions of game animals, and later all forms of wildlife, would grow.

After a year and a half of rest, Leopold was at last recovered enough to return to the Forest Service, though he was not able to return to the rigors of work in the field. He had to give up his position as supervisor of the Carson and was sent to an office job in Albuquerque. Here he began to develop a program for game protection and recreation in the national forests. He learned to understand the concept of *carrying capacity*—the ability of a particular area of land to support a certain amount of life.

He created a guide for foresters called *Game and Fish Handbook* in which he noted his emerging ideas about game protection, and he organized a number of protective game associations for sportsmen. He began putting out a newsletter for sportsmen called *The Pine Cone*, "to promote the protection and enjoyment of wild things." Through this newsletter he was able to educate sportsmen about the theory and practice of game protection. At this point, though he still saw the killing of predatory animals, or "varmints," as a necessary part of the program, he was beginning to develop an understanding of the interrelationships between the land, plants, animals, and humans.

The Forest Service wanted Leopold to come to work in Washington, D.C. But the bureaucracy of that city and the politics he would have to play were not for him. In repeatedly refusing to go, Leopold wrote to a supervisor, "I do not know whether I have twenty days or twenty years ahead of me. Whatever time I may have, I wish to accomplish something definite," and what he wanted to accomplish was game protection. And for this he felt he needed to be where he could *see* game.

So he continued to work for the Forest Service in the Southwest. By the end of 1919, he had risen to assistant district forester in charge of operations for an area that included 20 million acres of Forest Service land in that region.

By this time his interest in game protection and management had expanded to include land management as well. He was especially concerned with the problem of soil erosion, seeing so much of it in the overgrazed Southwest. He observed the increase in the number and severity of floods, and the change in the makeup of shrubs and wooded areas. Unlike most of his contemporaries, he connected this land damage with grazing behaviors. The idea that overgrazing was the primary cause of land erosion seems obvious to us now, but it was a bold assertion on Leopold's part in the early 1920s.

Though he had been schooled in the "wise use" theories of Gifford Pinchot, he was now moving beyond them. With his evolving awareness of interrelationships in nature, he was beginning to see a bigger picture. He now understood that in some cases, certain wild areas should be protected *from* use.

There were a few other people also interested in protecting what wilderness remained in the American landscape, but Leopold became one of the most vocal about it. He described wilderness as "a continuous stretch of country, preserved in its natural state, open to lawful hunting and fishing, big enough to absorb a two weeks' pack trip, and kept devoid of roads, artificial trails, cottages, or other works of man." He was concerned that areas meeting these criteria were quickly disappearing. "There is a limit to the number of lakes in existence," he wrote. "There is a limit to the mountainous areas of the world, and in each of these . . . there are portions of natural scenic beauty . . . which should be the property of all people."

He proposed the setting aside of the Gila Wilderness Area in a portion of the Gila National Forest. Established in June 1924, this became the nation's first official wilderness area. He mapped out the boundaries and asked that the government say "This is wilderness, and wilderness it shall remain." For his role in the promotion of the "wilderness idea," Leopold has since been called the "father of the wilderness system."

At 37 years of age, Leopold had achieved a great deal in his years with the Forest Service. He had been widely published in numerous journals and magazines and was considered a progressive thinker and knowledgeable researcher on such topics as game and wilderness protection and soil erosion. In fact, he was considered one of the leading spokesmen for the new field of wildlife management.

In the spring of 1924 Leopold accepted a transfer from New Mexico to Wisconsin to work for the Forest Service in the Forest Products Laboratory in Madison. Now the outdoor-loving forester was working with scientists whose job was to find uses for wood. He took the job with the understanding that he would soon be made director, but that did not happen. After four years in this position, he resigned from the Forest Service.

In the meantime he had not lost interest in either game management or wilderness protection. He saw game management as the necessary antidote to the problems created by humans upsetting the natural balances in the environment.

He spoke on wilderness at a conference on Outdoor Recreation in 1926, saying, "I am asserting that those who love the wilderness should not be wholly deprived of it, that while the reduction of wilderness has been a good thing, its extermination would be a very bad one, and that the conservation of wilderness is the most urgent and difficult of all the tasks that confront us."

When Leopold left the Forest Service in June 1928, he went to work as a game-management consultant. He was hired by the Sporting Arms and Ammunition Manufacturers' Institute to survey game conditions in the North Central states, including Michigan, Ohio, Indiana, Illinois, Wisconsin, Minnesota, and Iowa.

At last he was working professionally and specifically in game management. He traveled across the selected states, researching at universities and government offices, talking to farmers and sportsmen who had first-hand knowledge of game conditions. He found factual evidence to support theories, applying scientific method to a field that had never been seriously studied before.

After completing this study, he published his findings in a *Report on a Game Survey of the North Central States*. In it he sought to combine old ideas about protecting wildlife through controls on hunting with newer theories on management of the environment. "The purpose of this survey," he wrote, "is to appraise the chances for the practice of game management as a means for game restoration in the north central region. It attempts to describe game conditions as they exist, the opportunities which those conditions offer the human machinery available for acting on them, and the probable consequences of their neglect." Publication of this report in 1931 brought Leopold praise and increased respect from the conservation community, and it firmly established him as an authority on American game animals.

Drawing on research conducted in the Southwest and augmented by his findings in the *Game Survey*, Leopold produced a book called *Game Management*, which was published in 1933. It was the book that would give game management a scientific base on which to stand, and it would become the generally accepted textbook for the new field of game management.

It also helped lead to Aldo Leopold being offered the position of professor of game management in the Department of Agricultural Economics at the University of Wisconsin in Madison, a position created specifically for him, and which he would hold for the rest of his life.

The University of Wisconsin was already known for its role in the promotion of conservation. It was here that John Muir had received his (albeit limited) formal education in the natural sciences. The university was also known for its "Wisconsin Idea," the premise that the classrooms of the institution included all the land of the state.

As professor, Leopold's duties included the creation of a curriculum for the training of professional game managers. In this position he could both share information and direct research in the field that he was creating. In selecting graduate students for his program, Leopold looked for knowledge and experience in real-life field situations as well as book-learned knowledge.

In a paper entitled "Wildlife and Education," written in 1942, Leopold explained his philosophy of teaching. "The objective," he wrote, "is to teach the student to see the land, to understand what he sees, and enjoy what he understands. I say land rather than wildlife, because wildlife cannot be understood without understanding the landscape as a whole." Leopold believed that game managers had to be people who could see and understand the intricate relationships between land and living things.

He enjoyed taking classes on field excursions, often to the University of Wisconsin Arboretum and Wildlife Refuge, which he helped create, only three miles from the campus. He continually pointed out the things that he saw, things that the majority of people would miss. Often he would carry a camera, photographing both beauty and abuse as he saw it. These slides became part of his classroom teachings.

For some time since arriving in Wisconsin he had wanted to buy a piece of land to practice some of his theories of land restoration and management. In 1935 he found just the spot in an old worn-out farm in Sauk County. He purchased 80 acres immediately, and later added 40 more. He and his family (which now included he and Estella's five children) cleaned out the chicken coop and converted it to a rustic shelter that became known affectionately as "the shack." They used bits of wood washed ashore along the Wisconsin River to repair walls and window frames and to build benches and tables. At night there was plenty of singing and laughter and guitar playing around a campfire under the stars. Occasionally he brought some of his students there to observe and work on the process of land restoration.

Leopold's daughter Nina once expressed the idea behind the purchase of this piece of land. "Dad's selection of sick land as a place for his family outings was perhaps a new concept in recreation. The land our father purchased for $8.00 per acre had been abused, misused, destroyed. It had been carelessly lumbered, carelessly farmed, and carelessly abandoned. . . . And here was the challenge. Would it be possible to bring it back to health?"

She continues. "The marathon began. Over a period of 12 years, we slaved with our father and mother. We gathered seeds of native prairie grasses and flowers from nearby areas; we planted them among the old corn stubble. We planted native hardwoods and forest wildflowers and shrubs. We planted, then carried pails of water. . . . We learned how to nurture, how to care."

Leopold kept records of the plantings in his journals. He recorded that 95 percent of the pines planted in 1936 were dead due to drought within three months. Another year it was rabbits that attacked the seedlings. But he persisted, and after a dozen years of plantings, at least 8,000 new pines were growing on the land.

He learned a great deal from observing the changes wrought in the land over the years. He saw first-hand that though fire might destroy some plant life, it also served to clear the way for other forms. He saw that there were many factors that influenced the cycles of life and death and renewal in the natural world.

Leopold wrote of his feelings for this piece of land in an essay he called "Great Possessions." He begins,

The old chicken coop on the worn-out farm purchased by Leopold in 1935 became affectionately known as "the shack." Cleaned up, repaired and modestly furnished, it served as the rustic retreat from "too much civilization" for the Leopold family and friends.
(Author's collection, photo by Joseph Lucas)

Aldo Leopold

One hundred and twenty acres, according to the County Clerk, is the
extent of my worldly domain. But the County Clerk is a sleepy fellow,
who never looks at his record books before nine o'clock. What they
would show at daybreak is the question here at issue.

Books or no books, it is a fact, patent both to my dog and myself,
that at daybreak I am the sole owner of all the acres I can walk over.
It is not the boundaries that disappear, but the thought of being
bounded. Expanses unknown to deed or map are known to every
dawn, and solitude, supposed no longer to exist in my county, extends
on every hand as far as the dew can reach.

In 1935 Leopold participated with Robert Marshall and others
in the founding of the Wilderness Society. Concerned about the
increasing number of roads in national parks and other scenic
areas, this organization's founders dedicated it to the protection
of undeveloped land.

Leopold believed that wilderness had scientific value as a place
to study as well as spiritual value as a place to enjoy the beauty of
nature. For him wilderness was any place not altered by the
actions of people, and could even be a state of mind. Time and
again he warned that wilderness must be preserved because once
gone, it would be impossible to recreate.

During the summer of 1935 he traveled to Germany with other
conservationists to compare forestry methods. He found their
woods, among the most highly managed in Europe, sterile and
depressing with an artificial feeling about them and a lack of
wildlife. This experience added to his regard for the value of
natural wildness.

The following year he visited the Sierra Madre region of
Northern Mexico. He was overwhelmed by the unspoiled beauty
of this area, so close geographically to the Arizona and New
Mexico forests he knew so well, but worlds apart conservation-
ally. Here he at last realized that wolves and other predators
acted as natural checks and balances on other forms of wildlife
and he would never again advocate the extermination of any
form of wildlife. Of this land he would write: "It was here that
I first clearly realized that land is an organism, that all my life
I had seen only sick land, whereas here was a biota still in
perfect aboriginal health."

From this time on he focused more and more on the subject of
land health, and how, just as in human health, prevention—taking
care of the land before it was ruined—was the best policy. He

A view of the Wisconsin River as it flows past the Leopold property.
Maintained as the Leopold Memorial Reserve, this land serves both as a place
to learn and a place of quiet beauty, two of the functions of wilderness
highly valued by Leopold.
(Author's collection, photo by Joseph Lucas)

called for a new set of values among Americans, an attitude that would not condone or allow the abuse of land.

He called this attitude a "land ethic," believing that all people have the responsibility to nurture all that is beautiful in nature in every type of environment. A land ethic, he wrote, "changes the role of *homo sapiens* from conqueror of the land community to plain member and citizen of it. It implies respect for his fellow-members, and also respect for the community as such." He also wrote: "We abuse land because we regard it as a commodity belonging to us. When we see land as a community to which we belong, we may begin to use it with love and respect."

This experience also increased his fervor in calling for the protection of wilderness as a place to study land health, a place for comparison against the acts of civilization.

As his reputation in the conservation community grew, Leopold was asked to serve on a number of committees and commissions.

Aldo Leopold

One such appointment, as chairman of the Citizen's Deer Committee, involved him in a bitter deer controversy in the 1940s.

The state of the deer herd in Wisconsin at that time was bad; there were simply too many deer for the available habitat. The carrying capacity of the land, which he'd learned so much about in the Southwest, had been surpassed. To prevent the over-sized deer herd from starving and from destroying wooded areas, Leopold called for a massive reduction of the herd by hunting.

Repeatedly he called for an antlerless deer season, in which both male and female deer of all ages would be hunted. His advice was disregarded by those who feared this would overreduce the herd. Instead the deer suffered from disease and starvation.

In retrospect, he realized that part of the problem with the deer in Wisconsin was the virtual elimination of all their natural predators. Remembering the wolf he'd watched die in the Apache Forest, he wrote in a famous essay called "Thinking Like a Mountain": "I thought that because fewer wolves meant more deer, that no wolves would mean hunters' paradise. But after seeing the green fire die, I sensed that neither the wolf nor the mountain agreed with such a view."

Another time he wrote, "It would be unreasonable for foresters to demand wiping out the deer herd because deer eat trees. It is equally unreasonable for deer hunters to demand wiping out wolves because they eat deer." He called this change in attitude toward seeing the larger picture of the environment as a whole, "thinking like a mountain."

During the early to mid 1940s, Leopold began collecting some of these thoughts to be published in a book of essays. He considered a number of titles, including "Great Possessions," and began submitting the collection to various publishers.

With skillfully drawn word pictures, Leopold described the wisdom and beauty of the web of life. He chose various episodes from his life that served to teach a lesson, and very often that lesson was that all that is called progress is not necessarily good. He never said that it was necessarily bad either, only that we must assess the costs, see how what we are losing measures up against what we have gained.

In what would become the foreword for the book he wrote, "These essays are one man's strivings to live by and with, rather than on, the American land. I do not imply that this philosophy of land was always clear to me. It is rather the end-result of a life-journey, in the course of which I have felt sorrow, anger, puzzlement, or confusion over the inability of conservation to halt the juggernaut of land abuse."

He arranged the essays as they related to the months and seasons of the year, as in an almanac. He opens with "January Thaw," in which he writes,

In the July essay of A Sand County Almanac, *Leopold describes "a man-high stalk of cutleaf silphium." He lamented the destruction of roadside silphium, which he likened to the burning of books. This silphium grows undisturbed in the University of Wisconsin Arboretum, which Leopold helped create.*
(Author's collection)

Aldo Leopold

Each year, after the midwinter blizzards there comes a night of thaw when the tinkle of dripping water is heard in the land. It brings strange stirrings, not only to creatures abed for the night, but to some who have been asleep for the winter. The hibernating skunk, curled up in his den, uncurls himself and ventures forth to prowl the wet world, dragging his belly in the snow. His track marks one of the earliest datable events in that cycle of beginnings and ceasings which we call a year.

In "Good Oak," the essay for February, he writes, "There are two spiritual dangers in not owning a farm. One is the danger of supposing that breakfast comes from the grocery, and the other that heat comes from the furnace." To avoid these mistakes, he recommends a garden, and a fire in the grate of split good oak. He describes the history of the land he learns by examining the rings of a great oak that he cuts after it is killed by lightning. "We mourned the loss of the old tree, but knew that a dozen of its progeny standing straight and stalwart on the sands had already taken over its job of wood-making."

On through the springtime return of geese and sudden floods, the summertime blooming of wild plants, the autumn sound of geese and wind, to the tracks of animals in the snows of winter, he describes the beauty of each season of nature.

As he continued to teach his classes and work on the essays, sometime between late 1945 and early 1946, he began feeling pain in the left side of his face. As the pain grew worse, it was eventually diagnosed as tic douloureux, an inflammation of a nerve in the facial area. It caused him intense pain, eventually requiring that he be hospitalized in September 1947, for major surgery. Doctors had to drill a hole in his skull so that his brain could be lifted and the inflamed nerve cut.

Though he was able to return to teaching later that winter, the surgery left him weakened and he experienced some memory loss, especially with names. He also had some problems with his eyes, and was forced to lighten his work load.

In April 1948, he received the good news that Oxford University Press had agreed to publish his book of essays. A few days later, on Friday, April 16, Leopold, with his wife and youngest daughter Estella, headed for a spring planting session at the shack.

On Wednesday, April 21, Leopold was up early to count and classify the birds who greeted the sun so beautifully. Around mid-morning he noticed some smoke rising from a fire on a neighbor's property. The Leopolds drove in that direction to see how they could be of help. Leaving his wife by the roadside to guard against the fire jumping to his beloved pines, and his daughter to try to get a fire department to come, Leopold walked toward the fire with a shovel and pail of water. After a short while, he apparently felt a heart attack coming on. He set down his bucket of water and lay down on the ground with his hands folded across his chest. He died there of heart failure, most likely brought on by the tic douloureux.

Leopold's body was brought home and laid to rest in Burlington, Iowa. Numerous tributes to his life and his work were written by the many people who mourned his passing, but who seemed to feel glad that they had had a chance to know him.

Leopold's wife, children, and several friends worked together to see that his book of essays was published. Titled *A Sand County Almanac; and Sketches Here and There*, it was published in the fall of 1949. The book was immediately popular in the conservation community, reminding many of the people working so hard for the cause of the love and respect for nature that had inspired them in the first place. One fellow conservationist, William Vogt, predicted that the *Almanac* would be read "for decades, and probably centuries, to come," for it dealt with issues that would remain of interest as long as civilization struggled to control itself. It became one of the best-loved and most widely read environmental books ever written.

In 1953 another collection of Leopold's essays was published as *Round River*. In the title essay he had written, "Conservation is a state of harmony between men and land. By land is meant all of the things on, or in the earth. Harmony with land is like harmony with a friend; you cannot cherish his right hand and chop off his left."

Continuing, he wrote, "The last word in ignorance is the man who says of an animal or plant: 'What good is it?' If the land mechanism as a whole is good, then every part is good, whether we understand it or not. If the biota, in the course of eons, has built something we like but do not understand, then who but a fool would discard seemingly useless plants? To keep every cog and wheel is the first precaution of intelligent tinkering." All too often, he feared, "we do not yet recognize the small cogs and wheels."

Many of the essays in this book dealt with his hunting experiences, and some members of the conservation community as well as the general public have often had trouble with this. But for Leopold at least, the enjoyment of hunting was linked with the love of nature. For him there was no contradiction between the two. He always used hunting expeditions to answer some of his unending questions about wildlife, to increase his understanding of nature, and he always hunted (as Native Americans tradition-ally had) with the utmost respect for all living things. Some commentators have noted that perhaps this is an attitude that only those raised as sportsmen can understand fully.

In 1966 the *Almanac* was published in paperback with several of the non-hunting essays from *Round River*. With the increased awareness of environmental problems in the general public, the appreciative audience for the wisdom and poetry of the words of Aldo Leopold only seems to grow. Over a million copies of the various forms of *A Sand County Almanac* have been sold.

There have been many tributes to the memory of Aldo Leopold. The Sauk County farm has been preserved as the Leopold Memo-rial Reserve. At the University of Wisconsin Arboretum, where Leopold conducted many outside classes, a large stand of pines was designated "The Leopold Pines." Leopold had once written, "I love all trees, but I am in love with pines."

The Wilderness Society has had a plaque inscribed in his honor and placed at the Gila Wilderness Area, which he helped establish. It reads in part: "To Aldo Leopold, . . . forester and wildlife man-ager—outdoorsman—ecologist—philosopher and practical ideal-ist—interpreter of nature—pioneer in wilderness preservation. He taught an ethic of the land and by his teaching, his writing, and his example gave added depth, breadth, and insight to conservation."

Aldo Leopold was of course an ecologist, providing a functional approach to the environment as a whole. He saw that land is a complex interweaving of relationships between soil, water, plants, animals, and people. He was also a conservationist in the truest sense of the word, picking up where Muir left off in calling for preservation of the wild places. And he was, first and foremost, a naturalist, a man who saw and loved nature with a respectful, understanding love.

In his enunciation of a land ethic, Leopold satisfied his own definition of a prophet. In a tribute to a fellow conservationist Leopold had written, "A prophet is one who recognizes the birth of an idea in the collective mind, and who defines and clarifies with his life, its meanings and its implications." With his life Aldo Leopold showed us all the meaning of a land ethic.

Chronology

January 11, 1887   Aldo Leopold is born in Burlington, Iowa

1909   graduates from Yale University; hired by U.S. Forest Service

October 9, 1912   marries Estella Bergere

1924   Gila Wilderness Area established; Leopold transferred to Forest Products Lab, Madison, Wisconsin

1928   leaves Forest Service; works as game-management consultant

1931   *Report on a Game Survey of the North Central States* published

1933   *Game Management* published; Leopold becomes professor of game management at University of Wisconsin, Madison

1935   purchases abandoned farm; participates in founding of Wilderness Society

1936   visits Sierra Madre of Mexico; develops philosophy of land ethic

1947   hospitalized with inflamed facial nerve

April 1948   Oxford University Press agrees to publish book of essays

April 21, 1948   Leopold dies of heart failure while fighting brush fire

1949   *A Sand County Almanac; and Sketches Here and There* published

1953   *Round River* published

Further Reading

Works by Aldo Leopold

Game Management (New York: Scribner's, 1933). For many years, considered the finest work on this subject.

A Sand County Almanac; and Sketches Here and There (New York: Oxford University Press, 1949). Has also been reprinted in an illustrated version (1977) with photographs by Tom Algire and an afterword by Nina Leopold Bradley; and in paperback (1966) with some of the essays from *Round River*.

Round River (New York: Oxford University Press, 1953). Compiled from the journals of Aldo Leopold by his son Luna.

Other Works

Brown, David E. and Neil B. Carmony, editors. *Aldo Leopold's Wilderness; Selected Early Writings by the Author of A Sand County Almanac* (Harrisburg, PA: Stackpole Books, 1990). Describes the development of Leopold's thinking during his time in the Southwest by examining his published writings.

Flader, Susan L. *Thinking Like a Mountain: Aldo Leopold and the Evolution of an Ecological Attitude Toward Deer, Wolves, and Forests* (Columbia, MO: University of Missouri Press, 1974). Follows the development of Leopold's philosophy of land management, pointing out several critical turning points.

McCabe, Robert A. *Aldo Leopold: The Professor* (Amherst, WI: Palmer Publications, 1987). Written by one of the graduate students who worked closely with Leopold.

Meine, Curt. *Aldo Leopold: His Life and His Work* (Madison, WI: The University of Wisconsin Press, 1988). The most complete Leopold biography. Explores in detail his growth as a forester, scientist, writer, educator, philosopher, and conservationist.

Tanner, Thomas, editor. *Aldo Leopold: The Man and His Legacy* (Ankeny, IA: Soil Conservation Society of America, 1987). Essays on Leopold's work as a conservationist and related subjects.

Olaus and Margaret Murie: Voices for Wilderness

Olaus and Margaret Murie in 1959.
(Courtesy of Margaret Murie)

*T*he wedding was to have been on August 18, 1924. It was sometime after midnight, however, when the wedding party arrived at the little log church at Anvik, a small village on the shores of the Yukon River in Alaska. By the light of candles in the late (or early?) hours between the 18th and the 19th, Margaret Thomas married Olaus Murie, and together they headed for a honeymoon in the Arctic. She had traveled down the Yukon by mailboat from

Olaus and Margaret Murie

Fairbanks, where she'd recently been the first woman to graduate from the University of Alaska. He had traveled up from the Bering Sea where he'd been studying arctic birds for the U.S. Biological Survey. Now they were headed even further north to study caribou. Margaret would later describe herself as "the bride who happened to be along on the collecting trip," but she was much more than that. She was partner to a well-respected field biologist, and together Olaus and Margaret Murie would help educate the nation about the real value of this frozen land and work to preserve its beauty for future generations to know and love.

Olaus Murie was born in Moorhead, Minnesota, on March 1, 1889. His parents had just come there from Norway the year before. When Olaus was nearly 10 years old, his father died, leaving a wife, three sons, a house, a cow, and not much more. Each morning Olaus delivered pails of milk to neighbors before going to school. In the summer he was hired to work in gardens, at first earning only a few vegetables to bring home, and then later, as he grew, earning real wages. He and his brothers gathered wood in the nearby forest for stoves and fireplaces.

But somehow there was still time for pleasures as well. Nearby lakes provided swimming in summer and skating in winter. A densely wooded area in which the boys liked to camp was called "The Wilderness," and it inspired a great love and appreciation for the outdoors that would come to symbolize the life of Olaus Murie. Later he would say, "There were woods, birds, mammals. It was living close to the earth . . . Gee, it was wonderful!"

He read all the books on nature and wildlife he could find and enjoyed sketching the animals and plants of the forests and meadows around him. One day at Moorhead School a teacher pulled him aside and said, "Olaus, I want you to promise me something—keep on drawing!" Though he never formally studied art, he would continue to draw, and one day his drawings would be used to illustrate his own books and those of other nature writers.

When he was given the opportunity to work his way through Pacific University in Oregon, it was easy to choose to study biology. After graduating from Pacific University in 1912 he worked for a short time as a game warden in Oregon, until he was hired in 1914 as assistant to ornithologist W. E. Clyde Todd on an expedition to Hudson Bay. With two Ojibwa Indians to guide them, Murie and Todd traveled by canoe along a stretch of rivers and lakes in Northern Ontario. The scientific data gathered was important, but it was the wild beauty of the land, "the lakes we crossed, the rivers we went down, the water, the rapids, the inviting shorelines," that Murie would most remember.

These places so enchanted him that when the expedition was over in the fall he did not want to leave the North. He asked Todd to allow him to stay on and study bird and animal life through the winter. Though Todd could not afford to pay him a salary, he offered to help him sell any specimens he could collect. And so it was settled. Olaus stayed behind while his companions returned to the United States.

With an artist's eye for color, Murie described an October scene in his journal:

> *This evening was perfect. The water was smooth, reflecting the dull, deep gold of the nearest islands, the deep blues of the more distant spruce woods, and in the west one little daub of coppery red gleaming through the dark trees where the sun had gone down. . . . It was a fine northern autumn evening, which makes one glad to be alive and makes indoor work seem unbearable.*

Soon autumn changed to the deep, deep cold of winter and still Murie loved the northland. In late January he had his first experience of traveling by dog sled when he joined the mail carrier on a 700-mile trek to the village of Rupert House. It took four days, mostly spent running beside the dog-pulled sled, as much to keep warm in the sub-zero temperatures as because the load on the sled was heavy.

He joined team after team, heading progressively northward along the Quebec coast of Hudson Bay. In late April he made arrangements to travel with some Inuit to the Nastapoka River. The Inuit he was to live with spoke no English, and Murie knew little more than how to ask "what is the name of that?" in their language, but they got along fine.

When summer came he studied the nesting habits of birds as he made his way back toward more populated areas. In his journal he wrote of the long summer days spent exploring, writing, "the days were brimming with interest for me, the culmination of my long journey."

Two years later he was able to return again to northernmost Quebec with Todd, collecting specimens and information for the Carnegie Museum in Pittsburgh. By now he had grown skilled as a field biologist, and in 1920 he was hired by the U.S. Biological Survey and assigned the task of studying the habits of the Arctic caribou in Alaska and the Yukon Territory. He would spend the

Olaus Murie (left) with his brother Adolph, also a trained biologist, in Alaska. The brothers worked together during the study of arctic caribou and on other projects as well.
(Courtesy of National Park Service, HFC Historic Collection)

next several years engaged in this project. For some of the time he would be joined by his brother Adolph, who had also become a biologist.

On December 21, 1922, the shortest day of the year, Olaus was crossing an open stretch of tundra, barren, frozen, and yet beautiful in its own right. "These opens somehow impressed me profoundly," he wrote in his journal. "I thought of herds of caribou dotting such a scene. Certainly the wildness of it and the expanse of it seemed to require some wide-ranging animals and perhaps therein lay its charm for me. I seemed to want to roam over these plains myself, like the caribou, to feed on lichens, face the winds, and travel on and on."

During a break in the study, while visiting friends in Fairbanks, Olaus was introduced to a young woman who would soon become his life-long assistant, partner, and wife.

Margaret Thomas was born in Seattle, Washington, August 18, 1902. Her mother and father were divorced when she was young. Her mother remarried, and when Margaret was nine, her stepfather became assistant to the U.S. district attorney in the territory of Alaska. He went on ahead, and then sent for Margaret and her mother to join him in Fairbanks, a thriving mining town. The journey there by steamship, train, and sleigh was very exciting, and Margaret loved growing up in Alaska. She later said, "to an eager, curious child, everything was interesting there."

She describes the winters for us, saying, "When the thermometer went down to minus 20, and 30, and 50, and sometimes stayed there for weeks, the pattern of life was set—feeding the stoves. But, since the houses were small and low-ceilinged, and had storm windows and 'bankings' of earth about three feet high all around the outside walls, we were warm."

In the spring those bankings of earth would be covered with wildflowers. On the day that the crocuses first bloomed in the hills surrounding Fairbanks, school was let out for picnics and flower-picking.

Summer was when Christmas came to them because that's when the ice was off the Yukon River and its tributaries, and steamers sailed in with news and mail and packages from "the outside."

Mardy, as she was called by her family, left Fairbanks in 1918 to attend Reed College in Portland and then Simmons College in Boston.

Olaus and Margaret Murie

It was on a visit home to Fairbanks in 1921 that some neighbors introduced her to the young biologist, Olaus Murie. When neighbors invited the two young people along on a boat ride, Olaus showed off his animal mimicking skills, answering the distant call of a great horned owl. "Again the owl spoke," Margaret writes, "a bit closer this time. Olaus hooted again, and so it went until suddenly out of nowhere the dark soft shape floated into a treetop right above us on the riverbank and sat silhouetted against the golden sky. What kind of magic did this man have?"

It must have been magic indeed for though she was soon off to Boston for college and he returned to the frozen land of the caribou, when their paths crossed again the next summer, the two began courting and were soon in love. They made plans to marry, but Olaus knew that he would have to leave right after the ceremony for the caribou range. "Will you come with me?" he asked Margaret. "Yes, I want to go," was her reply.

Meanwhile Olaus had to go back to work, while Margaret stayed in Fairbanks to complete her college work there at the newly established University of Alaska. In June of 1924 she was the only graduate, the second graduate in the school's history, and the first woman graduate!

A few weeks later she was headed down the Yukon River, accompanied by her mother and her best friend. They were to rendezvous with Olaus near Anvik, where the wedding would take place. Margaret's friends had teased her when she packed her trousseau—a tent, snowshoes, a fur parka, and flannel pajamas. These were the things she would need, for their honeymoon would be spent in the north country in search of caribou.

A friend of Olaus's said to Mardy, "You go ahead and marry that fellow; he's a fine one. The only thing is, I don't know how you're ever going to keep up with him. He's half caribou, you know."

Margaret soon learned that the way to keep up with Olaus Murie was to learn as much as she could about his work. As they traveled up the Koyukuk River after the wedding ceremony, Olaus told her about "the little-known, teeming, rich life going on in the trees and streams, in the mossy tundra, and in the grassy sloughs."

"He explained the scientific reasons for collecting specimens of the arctic herd, for studying their food habits in winter, for observing their migration; it would close a gap in his previous three years' work of gathering facts about caribou all over Alaska." And as Olaus explained to her the scientific importance of his work, she heard the message behind the words as well, the great love for this vast frozen wilderness and all of its inhabitants.

Soon she had her "first lesson in being a field assistant to a naturalist"; Olaus instructed her in how to look for mouseholes. Though the caribou were the main focus of the study Olaus was conducting, he realized that in order to truly understand the caribou, he had to know about all of the life forms that inhabited the caribou's range, even the smallest of mice. "I learned that to the scientist these little creatures are interesting and important," says Margaret, "for they have a relationship to bigger creatures and to the land and are part of the great chain of life."

When they reached the settlement of Bettles, they transferred their possessions to dog sled and began the next phase of their journey. Sometimes Margaret rode on the sled, sometimes she drove it while Olaus ran, and often as not she ran beside it too. Sometimes as the dogs raced across the frozen land, she was thrown from the sled to land head first in a snow bank. Sometimes they slept in roadhouses along the way, but often their beds were made under the stars. One night, when she woke at 2 A.M. to see the moon shining through the trees, she tried to analyze her feelings. "As I lay there watching and listening, I felt somehow privileged, humble yet triumphant, waking so in the night hours, as though I had found omnipotence at work undisturbed."

The goal of this journey was the Endicott Mountains just north of Wiseman, the southern edge of the Brooks Range. Here they searched for information about the caribou and about the habitat in which it lived.

When they completed their work and headed down to Washington State, where Margaret's mom and stepfather had moved, Margaret was expecting their first child, so she remained there when Olaus headed out to study brown bears in the Alaskan Peninsula. By the time he returned, Martin Murie had been born.

When word of his next assignment came in March 1926, it was with pleasure that he was able to announce to Margaret, "We're going back up North." His mission was to study and band birds ("a *real* wild goose chase," Margaret called it) while traveling by boat along the Porcupine and Old Crow rivers in northeastern Alaska and northwestern Canada. Margaret was determined not to be left behind and began packing what she and the baby would need. A friend from Fairbanks, Jess Rust, would also come along.

When they reached Fort Yukon, where the Porcupine flowed into the Yukon River, they were told that they wouldn't have to worry about company when they got to the Old Crow because it "is the worst mosquito place in Alaska. Even the Indians stay out of there in the summer." But in the name of science, and armed with yards of mosquito netting, they went on.

Margaret would later recall that caring for the baby, and preparing and eating food without being devoured by mosquitoes, became an art and a science. A sense of humor and many hours of singing were key to saving their sanity. Olaus, on the other hand, "had a biologist's scorn of allowing anything biological to disturb him. All creatures are a legitimate part of the great pattern he believes in and lives by. He ignored the mosquitoes with a saintly manner"—which Margaret joked was nearly as irritating as the mosquitoes.

On June 21, 1926, the longest day of the year, they watched the midnight sun set on the Porcupine River on the Canada side of the border, 100-some miles above the Arctic Circle.

Despite a turbulent ride through rapids, an engine breakdown, and the mosquitoes, they were able to complete their mission and Olaus gathered important scientific information that would prove valuable in understanding this part of the world.

In the summer of 1927 Olaus was sent to Jackson Hole, Wyoming, to study the elk of the Grand Tetons. Martin, now two, had been joined by a baby sister, Joanne. A few years later Donald was born. While Olaus completed an exhaustive study of the elk, Margaret and the children were never far away.

Finding ways to amuse the children was never difficult. "They were busy from morning 'til night with places and objects they found right in the wilderness," says Margaret. When Martin grew a little older, he and his friends formed a club called "Gang of the Mountains." They explored, fished, collected and exhibited animals, and built treehouses.

A friend and colleague recorded that, "The Murie children were taught to be dependable and resourceful in the out-of-doors, for their father believed that all children need woods, waters, and wild creatures. When very young they learned how to camp out, put up scientific specimens, and band birds, as well as how to cut wood, spade, rake, and plant a garden. But there were always playtimes, too, full of sheer joy, mimicry, and foolishness, for Olaus also believed that the out-of-doors lost its real purpose if it were not a world of joy."

Meanwhile Olaus was trying to discover why so many of the elk of the famous Jackson Hole herd were dying. The problem, it turned out, was sores in the mouth caused by unnatural forage that led to infections and death. The unnatural forage, in turn, was at least partially the result of overgrazing by cattle and a disruption of the balance in the ecosystem due to the elimination of the elks' natural predators. The Biological Survey for which Olaus worked was in favor of the extermination of "varmints," such as wolves and coyotes. Olaus tried to protest, realizing that they were an important part of the ecosystem, but his words fell on deaf ears.

Despite the frustrations of dealing with bureaucrats who didn't understand field conditions, Olaus loved his job because he loved working in the wilderness. While there was often a certain element of danger, it was the special, quiet moments that truly meant wilderness to him. "This morning, for instance," he once wrote, "I stepped out of my tent, and in the dense fog which had settled over the meadow a great, dark form loomed up, came nearer, then slowly took the shape of a big bull moose. He walked slowly by my tent and . . . I watched until he melted away in the mist."

An elk bugling. Olaus Murie spent several years studying the famous elk herd of Jackson Hole.
(Courtesy of National Park Service, HFC Historic Collection)

There were also special sounds to be heard in the wilderness, such as the bugling of the elk in fall, the call of the wolf on a winter's night, the yodeling of a coyote in summer.

"These are the adventures of the wilderness," he wrote, "the scenes and the music which make up nature's great mosaic. I know when I have stood in nature's domain, rapt in wonder, in the presence of some manifestation of her charm, perhaps a sunset, a mighty unfolding of mountain ranges to the horizon, or the soft hooting of an owl in the dusk, at such times I have had my greatest peace."

During these years in Jackson Hole, the Muries thoughts were often on Alaska, and they worried about what would become of its vast wilderness areas. When the Wilderness Society was founded in 1935, the Muries were quick to join the efforts that group was making to preserve America's wild places.

When Bob Marshall, the society's principal founder and leader, died in 1945, Olaus was offered the opportunity to become its director. Olaus was ready to leave the Biological Survey, but he was not ready to move to Washington, D.C. Instead, an arrangement was worked out whereby he would be part-time director, and stay in Wyoming, and Howard Zahniser, as executive secretary, would take care of business in Washington.

The Muries moved to a log cabin on an old dude ranch in Moose, Wyoming, within the boundaries of Grand Teton National Park. Olaus's brother Adolph and Margaret's sister Louise, who had married each other four years before, moved into another house on the ranch.

Margaret remembers, "After Olaus became Director of the Wilderness Society and we moved to the ranch, the days were never long enough. Besides all the mountains of mail to be handled, on wilderness or other conservation matters, Olaus was working on his book *A Field Guide to Animal Tracks* and also at times doing illustrations for other people's books."

Suddenly the Muries were in the mainstream of the conservation movement, and at a very critical time, a time when bulldozers and dredges were preparing to "develop" many of the country's scenic places. Olaus argued that it was necessary for the wild places to remain empty of development in order to remain full of life.

It was work that demanded a great deal from them. "Correspondence was never quite caught up with"; wrote Margaret, "there were articles Olaus must write, lectures he must prepare, trips here and there and everywhere, to lecture, to meet, to confer, to testify, to teach, to persuade, to urge, to decide, to stand firm."

Their home became a mecca for the conservation movement. Their advice and support and friendship were much sought and cherished. According to Margaret, "Every conservationist or friend of a conservationist, every biologist or friend of a biologist, every schoolmate of our three children or friend of a schoolmate, who happened to be traveling through Jackson Hole [would] naturally come to call."

For peace and rest they had only to walk outside their front door. They always tried to get outside at least once every day for some outside activity—not going outside to get somewhere else; just going outside to be outside, to do something having to do with being outside.

When they moved to the ranch it had no electricity, just a temperamental old gasoline-engine generator that provided some power for light, sometimes. During the winter the roads were generally snowbound from December to April. Every two weeks the Muries would ski to where they'd parked the car by the highway, drive to town, buy fresh produce and other supplies, visit with friends, drive back to where they'd park the car, and ski back home, towing their supplies and mail on a sled.

During the 1950s Olaus was hospitalized for an extended period of time with lung problems. While he recuperated he worked on a book about his travels, which would become *Journeys to the Far North*. He also worked with Margaret on a book describing their life and work in Jackson Hole, which would be called *Wapiti Wilderness*. (*Wapiti* is a Native American word for "elk.")

In 1956 the Muries headed back to Alaska. They were hoping that a National Wildlife Refuge would be created in the Yukon River Area, a region of about nine million acres, and more scientific information about the land and wildlife was needed. Margaret's only hesitation was that daughter Joanne and her husband were waiting the birth of their first child. But her son-in-law pointed out to Margaret that it would be an honor for this baby (which turned out to be a boy) to be able to say that his grandmother had been on an Arctic expedition when he was born.

Olaus decided that they should study the valley of the Sheenjek River, a region that had not been explored extensively. Their party included several other scientists who would study various aspects of the area. Instead of traveling up the Yukon to the Sheenjek by boat, a journey that had taken the Muries two weeks three decades earlier, a small plane brought them in in a matter of hours, and set them on the shores of a lake they named Lobo, 150 miles north of the Arctic Circle.

The Muries found that they loved this land as much as ever. In a journal entry for July, Margaret wrote,

> We watched the storm clouds moving in, sliding over all the peaks, sending the advance streamers of mist up the middle of the valley. We felt the wind, and then the rain. And as we struggled on up the steep slope in the face of the storm, we both felt a real "participation." The environment is not tailored to man; it is itself, for itself. All its creatures fit in. They know how, from ages past. Man fits in or fights it. Fitting in, living in it, carries challenge, exhilaration, and peace.

In explaining why they were there she wrote,

> This area we hope will become an Arctic wildlife Range, so that one great representative unspoiled piece of Arctic wilderness can be kept as it is for basic scientific research and for recreation and inspiration for everyone who cares enough about untouched country to come and visit and leave it without the marks of man upon it. This is the value of this piece of wilderness—its absolutely untouched character. Not spectacular, no unique or "strange" features, but just the beautiful, wild free-running river, with no sign of man or his structures. For this feature alone the Arctic is worth preserving just as it is.

In his journal Olaus described the beauty of the Arctic flowers and the amazing way in which they literally "grow on ice." "The ice of the frozen ground gives off enough surface moisture to support a flourishing, varied flora," he wrote. "And what a lovely variety of blooms we have there, little and big. We can get the full appreciation of all this if we enter the Arctic humbly, with an inquiring mind, and look for the modest beauty to be found all about us."

It took four more years, but December 7, 1960, Olaus and Margaret Murie wept for joy upon receiving word that the Arctic Wildlife Range was established under the Fish and Wildlife Service with the boundaries they had hoped and worked for. To celebrate, the following spring the Muries returned to Lobo Lake and the shores of the Sheenjek one more time.

Olaus recorded this special "quiet moment" in his journal: "One day we came on a clearly defined caribou track beside a clump of purple saxifrage. As we looked at the blooming flower and the track of that arctic member of the deer clan, it occurred to us that here were a plant and an animal who had both found the Far North a fine place to live." As always, when the time came to go, they left without a trace of their having been there, except perhaps a few footprints of their own.

In 1962 Margaret's book, *Two in the Far North*, was published. In the preface she wrote: "My prayer [for Alaska] is that her great wild places will remain great, and wild, and free, where wolf and caribou, wolverine and grizzly bear, and all the Arctic blossoms may live on in the delicate balance which supported them long before impetuous man appeared in the North." She described her childhood in Alaska, her marriage to Olaus and the unique honeymoon they'd shared, and their visits to the Arctic over the years. She ended the book with the creation of the Arctic National Wildlife Refuge, which she called "one of their greatest joys."

Both Olaus and Mardy loved the Grand Teton Mountains of Wyoming, and devoted their lives to the preservation of such wilderness areas.
(Courtesy of National Park Service, HFC Historic Collection)

Olaus and Margaret Murie

Unfortunately, this great joy was all too soon followed by the greatest sorrow. On October 21, 1963, Olaus lost the battle he'd been fighting with cancer. Overwhelmed with grief, Mardy fled for awhile to Seattle, where her mother still lived. Finally she realized that "the grief and the missing would never go away, and I would have to build a life on top of it."

She returned to Jackson Hole and has since carried on the work of conservation. In 1964, Congress passed the Wilderness Act, which helped protect the wilderness areas of the United States, and which Olaus had vigorously promoted.

In 1977, while fighting for the Alaska Lands Act, which would set aside millions of acres of Alaskan wilderness, Margaret Murie spoke before a congressional committee. She had already been flown over the areas under consideration, as a consultant to the National Park Service, so that she could suggest the most critical to be saved. Now, at the age of 75, she was not afraid to admit, "I am testifying as an emotional woman and I would like to ask you, gentlemen, what's wrong with emotion?"

Eloquently she continued, "I hope the United States of America is not so rich that she can afford to let these wildernesses pass by—or so poor she cannot afford to keep them." When she finished speaking, she received a standing ovation. When the act was signed in 1980, President Jimmy Carter personally thanked her for her role in this historic legislation.

In the early 1990s Murie thought maybe it was time to leave the council of the Wilderness Society but was told that her support and participation were still as needed as ever in the face of talk of drilling for oil in the Arctic National Wildlife Refuge during the Iraqi crisis in the Persian Gulf. Even after the Persian Gulf crisis ended, pressure to allow drilling continued. Some of the land being studied for drilling is one of the main calving areas for caribou, which makes it totally incompatible with drilling. So Mardy Murie continues to fight against the spread of oil drilling in northern Alaska.

She continues to talk to young people, saying that "the most exciting thing I do is talk to the classes that come here to visit me from the Teton Science School; they give me hope."

She has been called "one of the most cherished conservation figures in the nation," a pioneer of conservation in every sense of the term. Her rapport with children has also made the name "mother" (or sometimes "godmother") of the American Conservation Movement fitting as well. A film depicting her life is being made by a group of filmmakers in association with the One World Arts Foundation.

From her home she continues to answer correspondence and phone calls relating to conservation work and to write letters to members of Congress. She believes strongly in individual responsibility. "Every citizen has a responsibility toward this planet," she says, and there is so much more to be done. She recently pointed out in a newspaper interview that "Only two percent of the land in this country is in the wild with legal protection. That is not enough. A great deal more should still be in its natural state."

There have been many rewards and recognitions over the years. Both Margaret and Olaus have received the Aldo Leopold Memorial Medal, the Audubon Medal, and the John Muir award of the Sierra Club. (Margaret was the first woman to receive the John Muir award.) They have been instrumental in the passage of the Arctic National Wildlife Refuge Act, the Wilderness Act, and the Arctic Lands Act. Together, they helped us see that what might have been considered nothing but a wasteland by some is in truth a great national treasure.

In *Journeys to the Far North*, published after his death, Olaus Murie wrote:

> *Mankind is still exploring. We are striving to find our way into the future. . . . We do not yet know where we are going, but it is important that we choose the right direction. To keep ourselves physically strong, to seek to know more and understand more through our scientific techniques, and to appreciate the beauties of the universe—these seem to be safe guideposts for us.*
>
> *We have been blessed with the power to appreciate beauty—in color, in form, and sound; we have been endowed with curiosity, the urge to reason things out scientifically, to wonder about ourselves and the universe. . . . Along with scientific search for truth, which must be paramount in all human endeavor, there is emerging an awareness of the poetic implications in what we learn.*
>
> *And I now also know how greatly privileged I have been.*

That would seem to be the answer to the question posed by his wife and partner, Margaret Murie, in her book, *Two in the Far North*, "What, after all, are the most precious things in life?"

Chronology

March 1, 1889	Olaus Murie born in Moorhead, Minnesota
August 18, 1902	Margaret Thomas born in Seattle, Washington
1912	Olaus graduates from Pacific University with degree in biology; works as a game warden in Oregon
1914 & 1916	Olaus travels to northern Canada for Carnegie Museum
1920	Olaus joins U.S. Biological Survey; begins four-year study of Arctic caribou
1924	Margaret graduates from University of Alaska; she and Olaus are married and travel to Endicott Mountains to complete caribou study
1926	the Muries and baby son Martin travel to Old Crow River in northwestern Canada to study birds
1927	Olaus begins study of Jackson Hole elk
1945	Olaus leaves Biological Survey; becomes director of Wilderness Society
1956	Muries travel to Sheenjek River in Alaska to study proposed Arctic Wildlife Range
1960	Arctic National Wildlife Refuge created
1962	*Two in the Far North* published
October 21, 1963	Olaus Murie dies of cancer
1964	Wilderness Act passed
1966	*Wapiti Wilderness* published
1973	*Journeys to the Far North* published
1980	Alaska Lands Act passed

Further Reading

Works by the Muries

Murie, Margaret. *Two in the Far North* (New York: Knopf, 1962). The story of Margaret Murie's adventures in Alaska, from her growing up in frontier Fairbanks, her Arctic honeymoon trip with Olaus, to the Old Crow and Sheenjek explorations.

Murie, Margaret and Olaus. *Wapiti Wilderness* (New York: Knopf, 1966). In alternating chapters, Olaus describes his work as a field biologist studying the elk of Jackson Hole, while Margaret describes their life together and the people around them. Illustrated with pen and ink drawings by Olaus.

Murie, Olaus. *Journeys to the Far North* (Palo Alto, CA: American West Publishing Co., 1973). Published from the journals of Olaus Murie after his death. Describes his field studies in Canada and Alaska.

Other Works

Bryant, Jennifer. *Margaret Murie, A Wilderness Life* (New York: Twenty-First Century Books, 1993). Interesting biography traces Margaret Murie's life from her move to Alaska to her current continuing efforts on behalf of conservation. Written for schoolchildren.

Wild, Peter. *Pioneer Conservationists of Western America* (Missoula, MT: Mountain Press Publishing Co., 1979). Explores the development of conservation in the West. Includes a very good chapter on Olaus Murie, as well as information on other conservationists, including John Muir, Aldo Leopold, and David Brower.

Marjory Stoneman Douglas: Friend of the Everglades

Marjory Stoneman Douglas with then-Governor (now Senator)
of Florida Bob Graham, at the Kissimmee River.
(Courtesy of South Florida Water Management District)

One day in 1942, 52-year-old Marjory Stoneman Douglas sat in the home that was also her writing studio in Coconut Grove, Florida. She'd come to Florida as a young woman in 1915 and had been writing about it ever since, first for her father's paper, the Miami *Herald*, and then in short stories that appeared in various magazines. Now an editor, Hervey Allen, was asking her to write a book about one of Florida's rivers, the Miami River, for a series of books he was working on, *The Rivers of America*.

Marjory laughed. "You can't write about the Miami River," she said. "It's only about an inch long." But here she had an editor asking her to write a book, and it was an opportunity she didn't want to pass up completely. So she asked if she could write a book about the Everglades and include in it the story of the Miami River. To her delight and amazement, Allen said okay.

Of this fateful moment she would later say, "There, on a writer's whim and an editor's decision, I was hooked with the idea that would consume me for the rest of my life."

———

Marjory Stoneman was born on April 7, 1890. Her father, Frank Stoneman, was a descendant of Levi Coffin, the Quaker abolitionist and leader of the Underground Railroad. Her mother, Lillian Trefethen, was of French and British descent. Her parents had met and married in Minneapolis, Minnesota, and Marjory, their one child, was born there.

When Marjory was three, her father's business failed, and the Stoneman family moved to Providence, Rhode Island, where another business effort failed.

Despite the rising tensions between her parents due to these financial setbacks and their differences in background and temperament, Marjory remembered her early childhood as happy. Her mother took her for lovely long evening walks and played the piano for her. Her father often read to her from *Hiawatha* and *Alice in Wonderland*. (She cried when Hiawatha stripped the birch tree of its bark, and she found it hard to accept the idea of a rabbit in a jacket with a watch. She called herself "a logical child," but she was capable of deep emotions as well.)

When she was four years old her parents took her with them on a business trip that included stops in Florida and in Havana, Cuba. She would always remember "the marvelous light, the wonderful white tropic light" that she saw there.

But the "bad things" that happened to the family, the financial problems, were too much of a strain for Lillian, who had a mental breakdown and took Marjory away with her to live with her parents and sister in Taunton, Massachusetts. The rest of Marjory's childhood was spent there with her mother, her maternal grandparents, and her Aunt Fanny, who were all very bitter toward Marjory's father, whom they blamed for Lillian's distress.

To escape the tensions of her family life, Marjory read a great deal and spent as many hours as possible in nearby libraries "looking things up." She says that it "gave me a great feeling of joy, knowing there was so much that I could put my hands on." She enjoyed writing too, and submitted pieces to the popular *St. Nicholas* magazine for children.

Marjory's mother continued to be unstable and when high school graduation approached, Marjory wasn't sure about leaving her to attend college. The two had clung together so closely all these years and Marjory knew her mother needed her. But as Marjory says, "[my grandmother knew that] even if my mother's life depended on my staying at home, my life depended on [my] getting away."

So Marjory enrolled in Wellesley College in Boston, only an hour and a half and yet world's away from home. She enrolled in a creative writing course and was at once established as a writer. She was also taught public speaking, or "elocution," and years later she would say, "I've been going around elocuting ever since."

Just before Marjory's senior year at Wellesley, Lillian underwent surgery for breast cancer. As soon as Marjory graduated the following summer (1912), she rushed home to be with her mother, who died a few weeks later.

Marjory got a job in a department store, first in St. Louis, Missouri, and then in Newark, New Jersey, but she really didn't know what to do with her life and just sort of drifted from day to day for awhile. While in this uncertain state of mind, having "no power of judgment over anything," she met a man named Kenneth Douglas. When he proposed to her, she accepted, not knowing what else to do, even though she knew almost nothing about him, and he was 30-some years her senior.

When Kenneth Douglas was arrested a short time later for some illegal business dealings, Marjory tried to be supportive for awhile, visiting him in jail and trying to pay the couple's bills on her own meager salary.

In 1915 her father, whom she had not heard from directly since she was six years old, sent an uncle to visit Marjory. Ned Stoneman convinced Marjory that she was going to ruin her life by staying with her husband and that she should go to live with her father. Frank Stoneman was living in Florida and had recently remarried. "It's time you knew your father," Uncle Ned said, and Marjory accepted the plan. At the age of 25 she boarded a train and headed for Florida. "I left my marriage and all my past history without a single regret," she would later write. "I was heading south with a sense of release, excitement, and anticipation."

When she arrived in Florida she saw again the bright tropical light she had first seen so long ago as a small child, and "recognized it as something I had loved and missed and longed for all my life." She was warmly welcomed by her father and stepmother, Lilla.

Frank Stoneman had first moved to Orlando, Florida, in 1896. In 1906 he moved to Miami and started a newspaper, the *Miami News Record*, which became the Miami *Herald* in 1910. With Marjory's writing ability she soon found work at the paper. "Suddenly, I found what I was meant to do," she said. Living in what was then a frontier town she found much to write about in the people and events of South Florida as she waited for her divorce and began to build a new life for herself.

One day during the summer of 1916, word reached the paper that the wife of a local plumber was about to be the first Florida woman to enlist in the war effort. Although, the United States didn't officially join the First World War until April 1917, the woman was able to join the U.S. Naval Reserves in 1916. Marjory was sent to cover the story, but when she called the paper a short while later it was to say, "Look, I got the story on the first woman to enlist. It turned out to be me." After spending an unhappy year in the navy doing office work, she joined the American Red Cross and went to France. Shortly after she arrived, World War I came to end and she witnessed both the joy of armistice and the tragedy of post-war misery. She traveled with the Red Cross, delivering powdered milk to starving people and writing about the relief efforts. In January 1920, she returned to Florida and to her job at the *Herald*.

She and her many friends would sometimes pile in someone's car in the late hours of the night for a trip to "the Glades"—the great vast marsh and swampland of the Everglades.

There were no roads through the Everglades at this time, but one had been started. (This road would be completed in 1926. It connected Tampa with Miami and became known as the Tamiami Trail.) Marjory and her friends drove out as far as they could, in the early 1920s this was just a few miles west of Miami, and parked. Building a fire there by the road, they'd watch the sun rise and the flight of huge flocks of beautiful Florida birds. "You could stand on the old roadway and look back toward a little bridge and see white ibis and wood stork sitting on the railings. You could walk over very quietly and watch the heron fishing."

At the time the future of the Everglades was being debated in Miami, as well as far away in Tallahassee, the state capital. Real estate developers were intent on draining the land and building roads and buildings on it. They had the ear of Governor Napoleon Bonaparte Broward.

Others, including Frank Stoneman, felt that the Everglades was a wilderness area that should be preserved. Marjory agreed, and she joined the committee, led by landscape architect Ernest F. Coe, that was working for the creation of a national park in the Everglades.

But the hectic pace of newspaper work was wearing her out and making her nervous. Still wanting to write, she quit the newspaper in 1924 and began writing stories for magazines. She had pieces published in *The Saturday Evening Post* and *Ladies Home Journal,* and the Sunday Magazine of the Chicago *Tribune.*

She did well enough with these that she was able to build a little house in Coconut Grove, a small town near Miami. While waiting for the house to be completed, she visited her aunt and grandmother in Taunton. During the time she was there, a terrible hurricane struck southeastern and south-central Florida, with

Douglas's first experiences with the Everglades included early morning picnics "to watch the sun rise and the flight of huge flocks of beautiful Florida birds." These birds, egrets and herons, were photographed in Everglades National Park.
(Courtesy of National Park Service, HFC Historic Collection)

93

hundreds of lives being lost in the area around Lake Okeechobee. Fortunately, her own little house suffered only some minor water and wind damage.

For the next decade she tried to divide her time between visiting relatives and friends in the North and living and working in her house in Florida near her father. In 1938 her last close relative up North, Aunt Fanny, died, and then her father died a few years later. She was now 51 years old herself, and finally feeling freed of the tensions she'd lived with since the separation of her parents.

It was at this time, when she was beginning work on a novel, that she had the fateful meeting with editor Hervey Allen. For the next five years she would focus her time and energy on the Everglades.

Douglas thought about what she knew about the Everglades. She knew that it was a wetlands area covering millions of acres and that it was inhabited by a multitude of spectacular birds and other wildlife. To find out more she paid a visit to Garald Parker, the Florida state hydrologist (someone who studies water). She asked him to describe the Everglades for her.

He told her that the Everglades was a place of shallow, flowing water in which tall blades of saw grass grew. When asked to define a river, Parker said that "a river is a body of fresh water moving more in one direction than the other."

After looking at a map of the Everglades, and thinking about what Parker had told her, Douglas began to have the idea that maybe the Everglades really was a river after all. She asked Parker what he thought of her idea of calling the Everglades a river of grass, and he agreed that it seemed to fit. And so Marjory Stoneman Douglas began calling the Everglades just that—a river of grass—and with this phrase she would change forever the way many people thought of that great wilderness.

She continued to talk to people who could explain to her the various aspects of the Everglades. She met with geologists, hydrologists, and archaeologists. She studied the work of horticulturalists (those who study plants) and ornithologists (those who study birds). She talked to people at local and state historical societies and she visited Indian reservations.

At the same time that she was working on the book, the final push for the creation of Everglades National Park was under way. Though Ernest Coe, the man who had worked so long and so hard for the park, was bitter that important parts of the Everglades ecosystem were not included in the park's boundaries, he was

By calling it a river of grass, Douglas changed the way many people thought about the Everglades.
(Courtesy of National Park Service, HFC Historic Collection)

present, as was Douglas, when it was dedicated in the summer of 1947 by President Truman.

A short time later, after five years of work, *Everglades: River of Grass* was published. The first chapter appeared in *Reader's Digest,* and the complete book was in stores in November 1947. By Christmas it was sold out. With the creation of the new park, public interest in learning about the Everglades was keen and the book was an immediate success.

Douglas begins the book by stating, "There are no other Everglades in the world." She tells that the earliest people to see them, the Indians of Florida, called them *Pa-hay-okee,* "grassy water," and the early English explorers put them on maps as "River Glades" or "Ever Glades," a glade being an open grassy place. Thus it has always been the grass and the water that have been the determining characteristics of the Everglades. She says that the

Everglades begin around Lake Okeechobee, and to the "south, southeast, and southwest, where the lake water slopped and seeped and ran over and under the rock and soil, and the greatest mass of the saw grass begins."

She describes the geologic foundations of the Everglades and the flora and fauna that inhabit them. She describes the people that have lived in and around the Everglades, from the earliest Indians to the coming of the Spanish conquistadores. She tells of the proud Mikasukis and Seminoles, who took on the power of the U.S. Army over and over again, and never were truly defeated.

She told of Governor Napoleon Bonaparte Broward, who, like the Frenchman for whom he was named, envisioned an empire. But his was to be "The Empire of the Everglades." He taunted the people of Florida that it would be a sad commentary on their "intelligence and energy" if they could not drain "a body of land 21 feet above the sea."

In 1905 the heavy machinery went to work. Rivers were dredged and canals dug. The limestone bedrock was dynamited. It was figured that a few cuts in the land would let all the fresh Everglades water drain out to the sea and the rich mucky soil would then yield bountiful produce by the bushelsful.

But it was not so simple. Indeed, some areas were drained dry. But then fires crackled and raged across thousands of acres of brown saw grass. "Fires spread crackling and hissing in the saw grass in vast waves and pillars and mountains of heavy cream-colored and purple-shadowed smoke," wrote Douglas. The rich soil blew away or dried up and hardened, and without the natural cycles of water and decay that the Everglades had known, the soil lost its fertility. During the dry season, salt water from the ocean flowed into the Everglades, poisoning wells and killing fish and other animals.

In short, writes Douglas, "The Everglades were dying." Much of its wildlife was endangered. As more and more fresh water from Lake Okeechobee flowed down canals to the sea and "flood control programs" prevented the sheet flow of water from the lake southward across the Everglades, the entire Everglades ecosystem was endangered.

Finally, in the 1940s, people began to take notice of the damage that had been done. "For the first time in South Florida since the earliest floods, there were mass meetings and protests, editorials, petitions, letters, and excited talk. Thousands, choking in acrid smoke, saw for the first time what the drainage of the Glades had brought to pass."

In the Miami area and along the southeastern coast, "people who had really become aroused, thoughtful people, residents and public officials worried at last about the water supply, began to see that it was never just a local problem, to be settled in makeshift bits and pieces. The Everglades were one thing, one vast unified harmonious whole, in which the old subtle balance, which had been destroyed, must somehow be replaced, if the nature of this whole region and the life of the coastal cities were to be saved."

Douglas said that the only two things that provided hope for the Everglades were "the large number of aroused citizens angrily insisting that something constructive must be done," and a scientific study of the Everglades that had just been completed. This study provided a report that recommended a variety of uses for the different areas of the Everglades. Only in the northernmost part of the Everglades was farming a reasonable use. The central area should be used for water storage and wildlife refuge. And the southern portion should basically be left alone.

That's what Ernest Coe had been saying all along. This was the area he wanted to preserve as Everglades National Park. He had been working toward that goal since the late 1920s. In 1946 a commission was established to begin buying land for the park, and in the summer of 1947 it was officially established. Douglas says of it, "It is the only national park in which the wildlife, the crocodiles, the trees, the orchids, [are] more important than the sheer geology of the country."

With the creation of the park Douglas closed the book on a hopeful note. "Perhaps even in this last hour, in a new relation of usefulness and beauty, the vast, magnificent, subtle and unique region of the Everglades may not be utterly lost."

With the royalties earned from *Everglades: River of Grass*, Douglas was able to continue to write, publishing a novel about people caught up in the Florida land boom of the 1920s, called *Road to the Sun*. She wrote another called *Freedom River*, about an escaped slave, an Indian, and the son of a Quaker family in South Florida. She wrote a book called *Alligator Crossing* for a series on U.S. National Parks, and a book called *Hurricane*, but complained that all the narrative about the tropical storms was cut in favor of scientific information. In 1967 her next most successful book, *Florida: The Long Frontier*, was published.

Throughout this period Douglas watched as drainage and development in the Everglades continued. The Central and South Florida Flood Control Project, adopted after further damage was done to cropland and cities by hurricanes in 1947, divided up the land and water resources among the many users. The project included levees and canals to separate the Everglades from the growing cities of the east and west coasts. It created five water conservation areas, or reservoirs, in the central area of the Everglades.

"Conservation of natural resources was among the officially stated aims of the project," Douglas would later write, "but before long it was clear that nature would be the lowest priority of the system's operators. They were engineers, not biologists—skilled at moving water, not at raising wood storks."

The problem, Douglas could see, was that "they did not factor in the sensitive responses of biology to human manipulation. The Everglades were not being destroyed wholesale, as they had been early in the century under the drainage boosterism of Broward [and others]. They were now declining by degrees. The changes would come so slowly that only the most careful watcher would notice them. But the changes were real."

In the 1960s, the U.S. Army Corps of Engineers began a project to "straighten out" the Kissimmee River. The Kissimmee meandered back and forth for a hundred miles before flowing into Lake Okeechobee. By straightening out the oxbows and draining the usually flooded wetlands along the river, the Corps turned it into a 52-mile canal with farmland on either side. What they created became known derisively as "the Kissimmee Ditch," and what they destroyed was a natural water filtration system and wildlife habitat.

Water that drained from the surrounding farmland now flowed more quickly down the river and into the lake. That water was laden with pesticides, fertilizers, and manure, and now there was no surrounding wetlands to filter those pollutants from the water. Lake Okeechobee was becoming increasingly polluted as the nutrients in these substances created an effect known as *eutrophication,* or oxygen depletion. The fishing industry on the lake and the food source for all kinds of wildlife were threatened.

In a new chapter added to a revised edition of *Everglades: River of Grass,* Douglas would write about the endangered wildlife.

By the 1970s, years of manipulation of the water had rearranged the seasons of drought and flood. The water managers presented a far worse threat than the hunters ever did. Two of Everglades National Park's most respected researchers, William Robertson and James Kushlan, concluded in 1974 that the legendary wading birds of South

Marjory Stoneman Douglas

Florida had been reduced by 90 percent, down to a shadow population of 250,000 . . . The ability of birds to show us the consequences of our own actions is among their most important and least appreciated attributes. Despite the free advice of the birds, we do not pay attention.

Then there was the plan to build a jetport on the edge of Everglades National Park. Douglas wrote, "The jetport would have destroyed hundreds of square miles of wetlands, directly or indirectly. It would have strung neon commercialism across the Everglades and brought fuel, asphalt, noise and garbage into the marsh." The changes in the water flow from Okeechobee had already caused monumental problems for the park. This new project would endanger the entire ecosystem.

Many local and national conservation agencies got involved in the fight. Joe Browder of the National Audubon Society asked Douglas to help. She wondered aloud what she as an individual could do. Browder suggested that she start a new organization dedicated specifically to the Everglades.

And from that conversation Friends of the Everglades was born. Douglas became president of the organization, which charged $1 for membership. Douglas began to travel extensively around central and southern Florida, becoming a familiar figure in dark glasses and wide-brimmed floppy hat. She took the fight for the Everglades to the schools and churches and civic halls. Under pressure from the combined forces of so many environmentalists, the plan to build the jetport was scrapped and Big Cypress National Preserve was created to protect an adjacent, related ecosystem. It was a major victory for "Marjory's Army," as she and her supporters were sometimes called.

Now in her late seventies, Douglas was just finding her true life's work. Of this she would write in her autobiography,

The Everglades were always a topic, but now they promised to become much more than that. They promised to become a reason for things, a central force in my existence at the beginning of my 80th year. Perhaps it had taken me that long to figure out exactly what I was able to contribute, and for me to marshall my forces.

At the same time it was decided that the Kissimmee River should be at least partially restored to its original channel. Douglas joyfully participated in a ceremony with Governor Bob Graham to throw shovels of dirt into the canal. She welcomed the "Save Our Everglades" program introduced by Graham in 1983.

Since he has moved from the governor's mansion to the U.S. Senate, and she continues to remind him to work for the Everglades.

In the late 1980s (as she neared her 100th birthday), Douglas became involved in the efforts to save the endangered Florida panther. When schoolchildren voted to name the panther the state animal she said, "they're going to have to be told that hunters are killing the panthers' food [deer and wild pig], and that the collaring program [to study panthers] is an outrage. Don't think I'm not going to tell them, because I am."

Douglas has received many awards over the years. In 1975 the Florida Audubon Society named her Conservationist of the Year. The following year she was similarly honored by the Florida Wildlife Foundation. In 1989 the Sierra Club made her an honorary vice-president, and in 1991 Governor Lawton Chiles signed a law dealing with a cleanup of the Everglades in Marjory Stoneman Douglas's front yard in recognition of her efforts on the Everglades' behalf. In 1993, just before her 103rd birthday, she was inducted into the Florida Artists Hall of Fame and in the fall of that year, President Bill Clinton honored her with the Medal of Freedom. When a production company in Los Angeles bought the movie rights to her autobiography, the reason they gave was that "she shows that a single person can make a difference."

In Key Biscayne, Florida, the Marjory Stoneman Douglas Nature Center was established as a place for people to learn more about the environment and about protecting it. Douglas is pleased to see people sharing her sense of responsibility toward the natural world. *Everglades: River of Grass,* which still sells several thousand copies a year, is required reading in many Florida school classes.

For all the work she has done on behalf of the Everglades, she very seldom goes there herself. "It's too buggy, too wet, too generally inhospitable," she says. "I suppose you could say the Everglades and I have the kind of friendship that doesn't depend on constant physical contact." It is enough for her to know how important they are to make her want to be sure that they are preserved.

"Protecting the park has become a high priority," she says, but "The Everglades Wars are not over." She decries the massive

In her nineties, Douglas became involved in efforts to save the endangered Florida panther, which there are only 30 to 50 left in the Everglades.
(Courtesy of National Park Service, HFC Historic Collection)

development of shopping malls and car dealerships where waterbirds used to nest. She fears that too many people still don't really know what the Everglades are and what their impact is on them. Douglas says, "so complete has been the mastery of the wilderness of South Florida that the place has been made safe for complacency and ignorance."

If the Everglades can be saved, and the verdict is not yet in, she believes that "It would be the first time that a region that has almost gone to complete ruin has been brought back by the understanding and wisdom of its citizens." And if that happens, the citizen most responsible will have been Marjory Stoneman Douglas.

Chronology

April 7, 1890	Marjory Stoneman is born in Minneapolis, Minnesota
1896	moves with her mother to Taunton, Massachusetts
1912	graduates from Wellesley College
1913	marries Kenneth Douglas
1915	joins her father in Miami, Florida; seeks a divorce; works for the Miami *Herald*
1916–19	joins the navy, then the Red Cross
1924	leaves the paper; writes articles and stories for magazines
1927	builds a home in Coconut Grove
1942	begins work on book about the Everglades
1947	Everglades National Park established; *Everglades: River of Grass* published
1950s–1960s	Douglas continues to publish fiction and nonfiction and to keep an eye on the Everglades
1969	Friends of the Everglades founded
1983	Governor Graham introduces "Save Our Everglades" program
1987	autobiography published
1988	revised and updated *Everglades: River of Grass* published
1993	Douglas, at the age of 103, is presented with the Medal of Freedom

Further Reading

Works by Marjory Stoneman Douglas

Everglades: River of Grass (Sarasota, FL: Pineapple Press, 1947, revised 1988). The book that changed the way people think of the Everglades. Besides describing the geology and biology, this book provides a history of people in the Everglades, from the ancient Calusa to the Seminole, and through the draining and development activities of settlers to current restoration efforts.

Florida: The Long Frontier (New York: Harper & Row, 1967). Examines the human and natural history of Florida, and shows how the two are interconnected.

Marjory Stoneman Douglas, Voice of the River (Englewood, FL: Pineapple Press, 1987). Marjory Stoneman Douglas's own account of her remarkable life and achievements, written as she neared her 100th birthday.

Other Works

Bryant, Jennifer. *Marjory Stoneman Douglas. Voice of the Everglades* (Frederick, MD: Twenty-First Century Books, 1992). Biography written for schoolchildren.

Lucas, Eileen. *The Everglades* (Madison, NJ: Raintree Steck-Vaughn, 1994). Describes plants and wildlife in the Everglades, the history of human activities in the Everglades, and the current problems and efforts to save this unique ecosystem. Written for middle- and upper-grade students.

Rachel Carson:
Ecological Writer

Rachel Carson at Woods Hole, Massachusetts, 1951.
(Photo by Edwin Gray, courtesy of Rachel Carson
Council, Inc.)

*E*arly morning bird walks had long been one of Rachel Carson's
special pleasures. She loved the sounds of the local songbirds and
the honking of migrating geese. She especially loved to be out in
the morning during springtime, when the dawn was alive with the
call of birds. It was hard to imagine a world without such music.
But lately Carson was concerned that such a dreadful thing could
come to pass.

Rachel Carson

She'd read about fields littered with the bodies of fallen birds, and coastlines covered with dead fish. There was a growing suspicion among some scientists and animal lovers that the widespread use of chemical pesticides was involved.

Then one day in 1958, when Rachel Carson was 51 years old, she received a letter from her friend, Olga Owens Huckins. Olga had created a private bird sanctuary, a place where birds could live and nest in safety, around her home in Duxbury, Massachusetts. The local government had decided to spray the area for mosquitoes. A low-flying plane sprayed chemical pesticide over the neighborhood, including the bird sanctuary. Immediately, the birds began dying. Within days dozens lay dead on the ground, their bodies twisted, their beaks gaping. Olga begged Rachel to find someone who could help stop the spraying.

Rachel Carson began to examine the evidence on pesticide use. The more she learned, the more concerned she became. Someone had to alert the public to the dangers. A trained biologist and successful writer with several very popular books to her credit, Carson had been considering a number of ideas for her next book. She knew now what the subject of her next book would be.

Rachel Louise Carson was born on May 27, 1907. She had a brother, Robert, and a sister, Marian, but they were eight and 10 years older than Rachel, so it often seemed like she was an only child while she was growing up.

The Carson family lived on a farm on the outskirts of Springdale, a small town some 11 miles from Pittsburgh, Pennsylvania. The farm was able to supply some of the Carson family's needs (a cow was kept for milk, pigs for meat, chickens for eggs), and Rachel's father, Robert Carson, was able to support the family with small real estate deals and various other jobs over the years.

The farm also provided a wonderful environment for young Rachel to grow up in, and was the place in which she first learned to know and love the things of nature. Many long summer days were spent in the meadow where she studied grasshoppers and butterflies, in the apple orchard where there were birds' nests to examine, and in the woods, so filled with plant and animal life. Whether alone or with her mother, who also loved the natural world, there was much for a curious, eager child to learn well before it was time to go to school.

When the time to go to school did come, she was as eager to learn there as she'd been in the woods and fields of home. She did well in school, though her mother frequently kept her home to avoid the various outbreaks of deadly childhood diseases. Thanks to her mother's tutoring, when Rachel returned to school after these absences, she was still able to shine as one of the best students.

When Rachel wasn't exploring the outdoors or studying her schoolwork, she loved to read and to write. Some of her favorite books were the animal stories of Beatrix Potter, and then later, the tales of the sea and nature by Joseph Conrad and Herman Melville, H. M. Tomlinson and Henry Beston.

At the age of 11 she had a story published in *St. Nicholas,* a popular publication for children. The next year she had two more stories published in the magazine and Rachel was sure that she wanted to be a writer when she grew up.

When she graduated from high school, she enrolled in the Pennsylvania College for Women in Pittsburgh with a major in English. There, she continued to enjoy writing and worked on the school newspaper.

Then, during her sophomore year, she signed up for a biology class, and her life would never be the same again. In this class she learned more about the things she'd loved all her life, and, though she thought this meant she had to give up all hope of becoming a writer, she decided that this was what she really wanted to study. She switched her major from literature to biology and graduated with high honors in May 1929.

She then spent the summer off the tip of Cape Cod, Massachusetts, doing marine biology work at the Woods Hole Laboratory. While she had always had an interest in the sea, this was the first time she actually saw it, and she found it as wonderful as she had imagined. Her work was mostly looking at tiny portions of turtle and other marine animal tissue under a microscope, but she also spent as much time as possible along the ocean front itself. Walking the beaches, climbing rocks, wading in tide pools, she was amazed and enchanted by the multitude of life forms to be found along the ocean's edge. She decided that marine biology would be her specialty.

In the fall she left Woods Hole and began her graduate studies in zoology at Johns Hopkins University in Baltimore, Maryland. She received her master's degree in June 1932, the midst of the Depression, and began the difficult work of trying to find a job. At a time when millions of Americans were out of work, jobs in science for women were practically nonexistent. The best she could do was a part-time teaching job and part-time lab assistant work. When her father died in July 1935, she knew that she had to do better as the sole supporter of herself and her mother.

She applied for a job with Elmer Higgins at the Bureau of Fisheries in Washington, D.C. Higgins asked if she could write. The Bureau of Fisheries had been asked to put together a series of radio broadcasts about fish and other marine life forms. They'd had a professional writer working on it, but he didn't know enough about fish. Then they'd had some scientists work on the project, but their writing was dreary. What they needed was someone with scientific knowledge who could also write well. When Carson submitted some writing samples to Higgins, he realized that he'd found just the right person for the job.

Rachel Carson went to work full time for the Bureau of Fisheries, which would later become part of the Fish and Wildlife Service. Her job was to respond to queries that had been received by her department. This involved research and synthesis of a great deal of scientific information. While performing her job very well, she was also increasing her knowledge of marine life.

One day she turned in some writing about sea creatures that Elmer Higgins said was too good. He suggested that she submit it to *The Atlantic Monthly,* a very prestigious magazine. When she finally worked up the nerve to send it in, she was pleasantly surprised to have her article accepted.

The article was entitled "Undersea," and in it she wrote:

Who has known the ocean? Neither you nor I, with our earth-bound senses, know the form and surge of the tide that beats over the crab hiding under the seaweed of his tide-pool home; or the lilt of the long, slow swells of midocean, where shoals of wandering fish prey and are preyed upon, and the dolphin breaks the waves to breathe the upper atmosphere.

After reading this article, Quincy Howe, an editor at Simon and Schuster, and Hendrik Willem Van Loon, author of *The Story of Mankind,* wrote to Carson and urged her to write a book on the sea. She later credited these two persons with motivating her to launch her career as a book writer.

Shortly after the death of her father, Rachel's sister Marian had died, leaving two young daughters, Virginia and Marjorie, for

Rachel and her mother to care for. Juggling these family responsibilities, her full-time job, and the work of research and writing,
Carson somehow managed to complete *Under the Sea-Wind*. In it
she told the story of life in the sea from the point of view of some
of its inhabitants. Arctic birds and baby mackerel were among her
cast of characters. Through the drama of the lives of these creatures, she shared the cycles of warmth and cold, light and dark,
that is life and death in the sea. In the foreword she wrote that this
book had been written "to make the sea and its life as vivid a reality
for those who may read the book as it has become for me during
the past decade."

Under the Sea-Wind received praise in both the literary and
scientific communities. But, on December 7, 1941, very shortly
after the book appeared, Pearl Harbor was bombed and the United
States entered World War II. Suddenly the attention of the nation
was on the war, and Carson's book was soon forgotten.

During the war she continued to work for the Fish and Wildlife
Service, writing about the value of eating fish and learning more
about the ocean. Later she worked on a series of government
booklets called *Conservation in Action* in which she discussed the
need to preserve wildlife habitats. She rose through the civil
service ranks to the position of editor-in-chief of the Information
Division of the Fish and Wildlife Service.

She still liked to be outside as much as possible and was pleased
when her work or excursions with the local Audubon Society took
her to new places. But wherever she went, she saw the sea. When
she visited the Florida Everglades, she wrote: "There was a curious
sense of the sea there in the heart of the Everglades." After a hike
in the Appalachians she wrote: "Perhaps it is not strange that I,
who greatly love the sea, should find much in the mountains to
remind me of it."

Carson really wanted to write another book about the sea, one
that would more fully explain what was going on under its vast
expanses. Scientists had learned a lot about the sea during and in
the years following World War II and she wanted to share this new
information with the general reading public.

The book, called *The Sea Around Us*, was completed during the
summer of 1950. In beautiful prose, Carson told the story of the
sea, from its theorized beginnings billions of years ago to the
everyday cycles of wind and wave, current and tide. She described
science's best theories about the beginnings of life in the sea, freely
admitting that many of the specifics remain a mystery.

Several magazines published parts of her book before it was actually printed. People were excited and interested by what they saw. When *The Sea Around Us* actually appeared in the summer of 1951, it sold out almost immediately. It quickly became a Book-of-the-Month Club selection and made it to the *New York Times*'s bestseller list, where it stayed for a year and a half.

It seemed that everyone loved *The Sea Around Us*. It did so well that *Under the Sea-Wind* was re-released and finally got the attention it deserved. Now Carson had two books on the best-seller list, making it possible for her to leave her job at the Fish and Wildlife Service and work full time as a scientist-writer. She was also able to buy a summer cottage near the ocean in Maine.

With the success of her books, Rachel Carson, a very private person, became a reluctant celebrity. She had stacks of fan mail to answer and invitations to consider. She was invited to speak at luncheons and meetings. In a speech she gave while accepting the National Book Award she commented that many people were

Carson's books about the ocean, The Sea Around Us *and* Under the Sea-Wind, *sold well enough that she was able to purchase a summer home near the coast of Maine. Here she was able to spend many enjoyable hours doing research for her next book,* The Edge of the Sea.
(Author's collection, photo by Robert O'Donnell)

surprised that a book of science should be so popular. "This notion that science is something that belongs in a separate compartment, apart from everyday life, is one that I should like to challenge," she said. "Science is part of the reality of living: it is the what, the how, and the why of everything in our experience."

Meanwhile, she had begun work on her next book, titled *The Edge of the Sea*. In preparing for this book, she was able to spend endless hours doing what she liked to do best—walking barefoot along the beach, examining and appreciating the diversity of life found there. She brought buckets of water home to study the tiny occupants under her microscope, delighting in their diversity of colors, shapes, and behaviors. She was always careful to return the water with its life back to the ocean, even if this meant climbing down a slippery rock cliff in the dark.

In *The Edge of the Sea*, Carson wanted to write more than a guidebook about the Atlantic coast. She strove to give readers an understanding of every aspect of the lives of the plants and animals that could be found there. In the preface she wrote:

> *To understand the shore, it is not enough to catalogue its life. Understanding comes only when, standing on a beach, we can sense the long rhythms of earth and sea that sculpted its land forms and produced the rock and sand of which it is composed. . . . It is not enough to pick up a shell and say "This is a murex," or "That is an angel's wing." True understanding demands intuitive comprehension of the whole life of the creature that once inhabited this empty shell: how it survived amid surf and storms, what were its enemies, how it found food and reproduced its kind, what were its relations to the particular sea world in which it lived.*

In other words, this was an ecological book.

She loved sharing this ecological approach to life with her family and close friends, especially with her niece Marjorie's young son Roger. She wrote an article about this for a magazine, later published as a book called *The Sense of Wonder*. When Marjorie died in 1957, Rachel adopted Roger, who was five years old at the time. Now she had a small child as well as her aging mother to care for.

Carson was considering several ideas for her next book when she received the letter from Olga Huckins. She knew that Olga's story about the death of birds from the spraying of pesticides was not an isolated incident. For a number of years such reports had been coming in. But few people wanted to listen. Carson had once offered to do an article on the dangers of pesticide use for a national magazine but the offer was rejected. She was now determined, however, that this story would be told.

The pesticide used in Duxbury contained the chemical DDT (dichloro-diphenyl-trichloroethane), a humanmade chemical in the chlorohydrocarbon family. DDT had been used to kill lice on soldiers during World War II. After the war DDT and a number of other chemical pesticides became widely used in the newly declared war on insects. *Popular Science* magazine reported that "At last science has found the weapons for total victory on the insect front."

Government agencies in the United States and in other countries were out to eliminate pests of many kinds, ranging from crop-damaging insects in agricultural areas to the nuisance of mosquitoes in suburban neighborhoods. The chemical industry boomed, and this was good for the economy. Chemical companies insisted that pesticides were harmless to people and "good" animals. But they had no research to back this up, and there was much visible evidence to the contrary.

Part of the problem was that no one seemed to be looking at the big picture. No one questioned how mosquitoes and ants and other insects fit into the total ecology, what kind of relationships they might have with other insects and other animals. No one asked the difficult questions that Rachel Carson was now asking about costs to humans, animals, and the environment in the use of these chemicals.

One of the problems with chlorinated hydrocarbons is the way they become more concentrated in living tissues as they move up the food chain. Thus, minute traces in small plants become slightly larger amounts in small animals that eat them, and can reach very large concentrations in larger animals that feed on small ones. Also, they take a long time to break down in the environment, and they leave harmful residues behind. They last so long that they are now found in virtually all parts of the world. Traces of DDT have been found in shellfish caught 100 miles out at sea, in seals and penguins in the Antarctic, and in human mother's milk.

As Carson was deeply involved in work on this new book, she suffered several personal setbacks. In December 1958, her mother died. A college friend of Rachel's had described Maria Carson as "a brilliant woman." She had encouraged Rachel to wonder about and observe and identify the things of nature. She had been very supportive of this book on pesticides.

Rachel herself was not feeling well either. There were numerous minor ailments (flu, sinus infections, an ulcer), and then in 1960

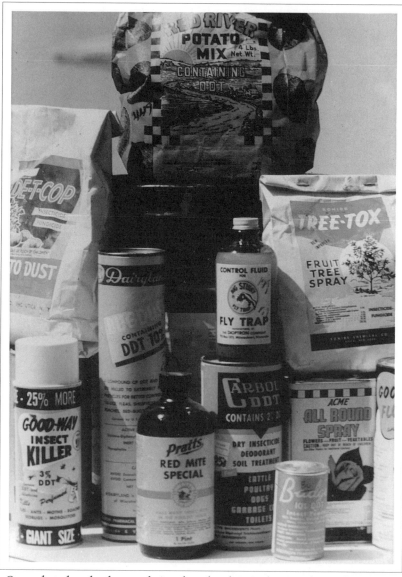

Once alerted to the damage being done by chemical pesticides such as DDT, Carson was determined to share this information with the public.
(Courtesy of Wisconsin Department of Natural Resources)

it was discovered that she had breast cancer. Determined to fight it as best she could, she underwent surgery and radiation treatment. Often she was forced to work in bed when she was not well enough to get up. She was determined to complete this book, however, knowing that it was very important work.

The new book would be called *Silent Spring*, a phrase that dramatically symbolized the dangerous results of the widespread use of chemical poisons. In the opening chapter she described what appeared at first to be an average American town. But then she says:

> *a strange blight crept over the area and everything began to change. . . . Mysterious maladies swept the flocks of chickens; the cattle and sheep sickened and died. Everywhere was a shadow of death. . . . There was a strange stillness. . . . On the mornings that had once throbbed with the dawn chorus of robins, catbirds, doves, jays, wrens, and scores of other bird voices there was now no sound; only silence lay over the fields and woods and marsh.*

Carson goes on to tell her readers that these things have already happened in some places, though not all at once in any one place. As to what has caused these terrible and mysterious occurrences, she says: "No witchcraft, no enemy action had silenced the rebirth of new life in this stricken world. The people had done it to themselves."

In following chapters she describes the increase in use of chemical pesticides in the years following World War II. She describes the pesticides themselves and some of the things that have happened as a result of their use. She describes the aftermath of pesticide spraying intended to kill Japanese beetles in a small town in Illinois.

> *As the chemical penetrated the soil the poisoned beetle grubs crawled out on the surface of the ground, where they remained for some time before they died, attractive to insect-eating birds. . . . Brown thrashers, starlings, meadowlarks, grackles, and pheasants were virtually wiped out. . . . Birds seen drinking in puddles left by rain a few days after the spraying were inevitably doomed.*

She cited another example of DDT spraying in Long Island, New York. She wrote: "They sprayed truck gardens and dairy farms, fish ponds and salt marshes. They sprayed the quarter-acre lots of suburbia, drenching a housewife, . . . and showering insecticide over children at play and commuters at railway stations. . . . A fine quarter horse drank from a trough in a field which the planes had sprayed; ten hours later it was dead." All this was part of an effort to eliminate the gypsy moth, a forest insect.

Instead of eliminating insect pests however, the use of pesticides often results in more resistant insect populations. Carson wrote: "Under the stress of intensive chemical spraying the weaker members of the insect populations are being weeded out. Now, in many areas and among many species only the strong and fit remain to defy our efforts to control them."

She touched on the subject of the dangers to human health due to chemical pesticide use. Though much more study on this subject was needed, enough was known to warrant a warning that increased caution was needed.

In her final chapter she presents an alternative to the use of such poisons. She describes numerous biological solutions to insect and pest problems. These biological solutions are "based on understanding of the living organisms they seek to control, and of the whole fabric of life to which these organisms belong." In the opening chapter she had clearly stated that she was *not* saying that there was no insect problem in need of control. What she was saying was that "control must be geared to realities, not mythical situations, and that the methods employed must be such that they do not destroy us along with the insects."

In June 1962 a condensed form of the book appeared in *The New Yorker*. (The book itself became available in September.) Opponents of the work (supporters of the chemical industry and many government officials, particularly in the Department of Agriculture) wasted no time expressing their displeasure.

The chemical industry decided to attack the author personally. They called her names like "nature nut," "hysterical," and more. They accused Carson of being emotional, when they in fact were being emotional and irrational in their attack on her. They hollered "distortion" and "inaccuracy," but they seldom were specific about what information they thought was distorted or innacurate. They argued with statements she had never made.

They reacted as if she had called for an immediate ban on any use of chemical pesticides, which she most emphatically did not. They predicted worldwide famine and anarchy if chemical pesticides were restricted in any way. They accused her of being one-sided, when they had always been one-sided in their glorifications of chemical pesticides.

In *Silent Spring* Carson presented the side of the story that the public had not heard before. She cited a great deal of factual information; at the back of the book are over 50 pages of source notes. She built her case on a solid foundation of facts, and all but a few minor statements were able to withstand the close, and often brutal, scrutiny.

One ecologist compared the impact of *Silent Spring* on the pesticide industry with the effect Upton Sinclair's book *The Jungle* had had on the meat packing industry. It was compared to Charles Darwin's *Origin of Species* for its impact on the scientific community. On the general public, its results were similar to that of Harriet Beecher Stowe's *Uncle Tom's Cabin*. It opened the eyes of countless numbers of individuals to what was going on around them. And once their eyes were opened, they began asking questions about chemical pesticides and other toxic pollutants in the environment, and began learning what they could do about it.

In April 1963, Carson appeared on a special television news program called "The Silent Spring of Rachel Carson." It was an opportunity for both sides of the controversy to express their views. Carson felt satisfied that she calmly presented the facts as she understood them and that she'd given the public solid information to think about. She reiterated that: "It is not my contention that chemical pesticides must never be used. I do contend that we have allowed these chemicals to be used with little or no advance investigation of their effect on soil, water, and man himself." She summed up her position by adding that "We still talk in terms of conquest. . . . But man is a part of nature and his war against nature is inevitably a war against himself."

Immediately after the book appeared, President Kennedy had ordered a scientific study of chemical pesticide use. In May of 1963, the President's Science Advisory Committee issued their report, acknowledging that: "Until the publication of *Silent Spring* by Rachel Carson, people were generally unaware of the toxicity of pesticides." This report was one of the first government documents to say anything negative about pesticides, and showed that the book was achieving its twofold purpose: to inform the public about the facts regarding pesticides, and to prompt the government to take action.

A Senate subcommittee (known as the Ribicoff Committee) was established to review all federal programs dealing with pollution and environmental hazards. Within months of the book's publication, more than 40 pieces of legislation dealing with pesticide use were being considered by state governments across the nation, and political candidates were asking Carson for advice on pesticide issues.

The next year the U.S. Department of Agriculture (USDA) changed its regulatory policy from one in which someone with a concern had to prove that a chemical was harmful, to one in which the manufacturer had to prove that the chemical was safe.

There were also rewards in the form of awards and recognition. In January 1963, she was proud to accept the Schweitzer Medal of the Animal Welfare Institute, as she greatly admired Dr. Albert Schweitzer and his attitude of "reverence for life." In March she received the Conservationist of the Year award from the National Wildlife Federation.

That summer she was relieved to retreat somewhat from the controversy for a few happy months in Maine. Weakened by illness, unable to do much hiking and climbing, she spent many hours on her porch, or on a blanket on the beach, absorbing the beauty of the seacoast. She still took great pleasure in watching the pageantry of life under her microscope.

In October, though confined to a wheelchair, she was able to visit California to see the giant redwoods and Muir Woods, accompanied by Sierra Club Director David Brower. In December there were awards and recognitions in New York. But she was losing her battle with cancer, and she knew that she did not have much time left. She wrote to a friend, "now every month, every day is precious." But she could listen to the songbirds she loved so well and know that she had done her best to help them. She died at home on April 14, 1964.

Rachel Carson has been called the founder of the modern ecology movement. She was concerned about the big picture—about the relationships between all living things and their environment, about the abuse of the natural world. She said that her motivation for writing *Silent Spring* was the same as for all her books: "In each of my books I have tried to say that all the life of the planet is interrelated, that each species has its own ties to others, and that all are related to the earth."

She opened the eyes of many to the wonders of the sea. The author Hendrik Van Loon, who had prompted her to write a book about the sea, told her that before he'd read *The Sea Around Us* he'd been impressed with the emptiness of the ocean's surface. Thanks to her he was reminded that the ocean is anything but empty. Her books about the ocean combined the scientist's facts with the poet's vision. They brought joy and information to many.

But she is most remembered for *Silent Spring*, the book that opened the eyes of many to the dangers of chemical poisons. As Frank Graham Jr. says, "Rachel Carson uncovered the hiding places of facts that should have been disclosed to the public long before; she broke the information barrier."

Thanks largely to this book, the use of DDT was banned in the United States. Laws were passed requiring chemical companies to test their products and monitor their effects on the environment. In 1970 the Environmental Protection Agency was created in response to the activism that had become more vocal and more focused since the publication of *Silent Spring*.

Many individuals became much more careful about their use of dangerous chemicals. The publication of *Silent Spring* and the discussions it provoked inspired the government to take action against many forms of air and water pollution much more quickly than it otherwise would have. As a society, we will never again be so innocent in our use of such poisons.

But the battle is not over. Still today the World Health Organization reports that millions of human poisonings occur each year from pesticides. Thousands of people died in Bhopal, India when a gas used in the manufacture of pesticides escaped into the air.

We need to continue to explore the use of biological pest controls. For example, beneficial insects, such as ladybugs, can be used to control certain harmful insects. Particular viruses and bacteria that attack harmful insects may also be used. And crop rotation and timed planting are farming techniques that can reduce the threat of insect attacks. Consumers can help by increasing the demand for produce grown without the use of chemicals.

Shortly before she died Rachel Carson said, "Conservation is a cause that has no end. There is no point at which we will say 'our work is finished.'" To carry on her efforts, The Rachel Carson Council was established to serve as a bridge between concerned individuals and the scientific community.

When the Presidential Medal of Freedom, the highest civilian award given in the United States, was presented to Roger Christie on behalf of Rachel Carson, Jimmy Carter said, "Always concerned, always eloquent, she created a tide of environmental consciousness that has not ebbed."

Chronology

May 27, 1907	Rachel Carson is born in Springdale, Pennsylvania
May 1929	graduates from Pennsylvania College for Women
summer 1929	works at Woods Hole Laboratory
June 1932	receives master's degree in zoology from Johns Hopkins University
1935	starts at the Bureau of Fisheries
1937	publishes "Undersea" in *The Atlantic Monthly*
1941	*Under the Sea-Wind* published
1951	*The Sea Around Us* published
1955	*The Edge of the Sea* published
1956	*The Sense of Wonder* published
1957	Carson adopts her grand-nephew
1960	diagnosed with cancer
1962	excerpts from *Silent Spring* published in *The New Yorker* in June, complete book published in September
January 1963	Carson receives the Schweitzer Medal of the Animal Welfare Institute
March 1963	receives the Conservationist of the Year award from the National Wildlife Federation
April 1963	appears on television in "The Silent Spring of Rachel Carson"
May 1963	President's Science Advisory Committee recommends an investigation of environmental hazards
April 14, 1964	dies of cancer at age 57

Further Reading

Works by Rachel Carson

Under the Sea-Wind (New York: Oxford University Press, 1941). Carson describes life in the sea.

The Sea Around Us (New York: Oxford University Press, 1951). Detailed look at the geology and biology of the ocean.

The Edge of the Sea (Boston, MA: Houghton Mifflin, 1955). Carson describes the interrelationships between life forms to be found along the shores of the Atlantic Ocean from Maine to Florida.

The Sense of Wonder (New York: Harper & Row, 1956). Shows how to share a natural wonder for the things of nature.

Silent Spring (Greenwich, CT: Fawcett, 1962). Considered one of the most important environmental books ever written, this book describes the dangers of thoughtless use of chemical pesticides.

Other Works

Brooks, Paul. *The House of Life, Rachel Carson at Work* (Boston, MA: Houghton Mifflin, 1972). Carson's editor describes what it was like for her to write each of her books.

————. *Speaking for Nature* (Boston, MA: Houghton Mifflin, 1980). Tells how writing naturalists have influenced the thinking of Americans toward nature.

Graham, Frank Jr. *Since Silent Spring* (Boston, MA: Houghton Mifflin, 1970). The author examines the results of *Silent Spring* in light of the controversial response to its publication.

Jezer, Marty. *Rachel Carson, Biologist and Author* (New York: Chelsea House, 1988). Insightful biography for young adult and student readers.

Wadsworth, Ginger. *Rachel Carson* (Minneapolis, MN: Lerner Publications, 1992). Easy-to-read biography for young adults. Includes epilogue, list of conservation organizations, photos.

David Brower:
"Preaching" for the Earth

David Brower in 1991.
(Courtesy of Earth Island Institute)

*O*n a sheer mountain slope in the Sierra Nevada, 21-year-old David Brower carefully made his way along a rocky ledge. It was summertime, 1933, though here in the high reaches of these mighty peaks there was a fresh dusting of snow that made the going a bit more slippery.

Brower was in the midst of a seven-week backpacking trip, financed with $21 he had earned working on a cousin's farm the previous spring. Since discovering the sport of mountaineering a few summers before, Brower had spent as much time as possible engaged in it, finding himself especially drawn to the Sierra Nevada, the "Range of Light," that had so inspired John Muir a century before. He read Muir's accounts of his adventures in the Sierra and understood what Muir meant when he wrote: "I am always glad to touch the living rock again and dip my head in high mountain air."

Brower reached up and grabbed a rock overhead, planning to use it to pull himself up the mountain's sheer side. Suddenly, as he hung from the rock with both arms raised, it gave way. Only a quick grab at a nearby ledge saved him from what probably would have been a deadly 75-foot fall.

This brush with death did not deter Brower from climbing, but it did encourage him to be more careful about testing rocks before putting his weight on them. In the years to come he would make many "first ascents" of even more difficult and dangerous peaks. He would learn to use pitons (spikes with holes like the eye of a needle) and ropes to make climbing safer.

It was his experiences in mountaineering, his appreciation of the beauty of wild places, and his desire to protect these wild places for future generations, that led Brower to a career as an activist and conservationist.

David Brower was born July 1, 1912, in Berkeley, California, when that was just a small college town across the bay from San Francisco. His father was an instructor of mechanical drawing. His parents loved to take David (and his older brother and sister, Ralph and Edith) for walks in the low hills around Berkeley and in the high mountains of the Sierra Nevada.

David enjoyed being outside as much as possible. Following the flight of butterflies through meadows and climbing on Founders Rock near the college campus provided hours of fun and freedom. He found that with rocks and sticks he could back up the water of Strawberry Creek, and then enjoy the surge of water back into the streambed when the obstruction was removed.

He learned to love animals after his mother read him *The Adventures of Bobby Coon,* by Thornton W. Burgess, and later, when he read *Wild Animals I Have Known* by Ernest Thompson Seton. He credits these authors and their books with having a hand in his becoming a conservationist.

After the birth of her youngest child, Joe, in 1920, Brower's mother lost her sight, and it became one of David's greatest pleasures to guide her on walks and describe for her the beauty of nature she loved but could no longer see. Years later when David would write of the beautiful places he was able to visit, he said he was still writing as much for her as for himself.

About the same time his mother lost her sight, his father lost his job and family finances were extremely strained. Everyone had to pitch in. Dave delivered newspapers and worked to maintain the rental apartments that helped sustain the family.

In 1930 he took a summer job at Berkeley's Echo Lake camp. One of his duties was to guide campers up the mountains above the lake, and he gradually became a skilled mountain climber. He was also able to share additional trips in the Sierra Nevada with his family and before long he was hooked on mountaineering. He read John Muir's *My First Summer in the Sierra* and Clarence King's *Mountaineering in the Sierra Nevada,* reveling in the tales of mountain beauty and adventure.

Brower attended the University of California in Berkeley for awhile but dropped out in his second year. Someone told Brower that since he liked the mountains so much he ought to check out the Sierra Club. He began buying back issues of the club's annual newsletter, the *Sierra Club Bulletin.* Brower was captivated by the stories of individual climbing trips in the mountains and by the beautiful photos taken by Ansel Adams. On one of his own hiking trips he met the renowned photographer, and the two hiking enthusiasts became friends. In 1933, Richard Leonard, another accomplished hiker, sponsored Brower's membership in the club.

Brower spent some time training with other climbers and learned a lot about safety. After several summers of climbing, he began to put his thoughts and experiences into words and submitted some of these pieces to the *Bulletin.* In 1935 his description of a climbing excursion, "Far from the Madding Mules" was published and shortly thereafter he became an unpaid member of the *Bulletin's* editorial board. Here he sharpened his skills in editing and learned more about publishing while working on a subject he loved dearly—mountaineering.

He described in the article that he suddenly realized at the end of the trip when he was returning to Berkeley that he "was not coming home—he had just left it!"

Of these summer hiking trips he would say, "The energy I expended certainly awakened me to wilderness and enabled me to go to some places on the map that white man had not visited before. . . . But I had not yet understood what wilderness means or what the threats to it were."

After returning from an expedition to Canada's Mount Waddington in 1935, Brower was hired by the Yosemite Park & Curry Company, which operated the concessions in Yosemite Valley. The job was in the accounting office, which he did not like, but the location was in Yosemite Valley, which he did like. Soon he was working in the publicity department, taking pictures of park visitors for their hometown newspapers, as part of the company's program to bring more visitors to the park.

As Brower says, "There were two problems [with this]. First, I was more interested in photographing scenery than people. . . . Second, I was not anxious to see Yosemite more crowded than it already was." The best part about the job as far as Brower was concerned was the opportunity to work with and learn from Ansel Adams who had a studio there.

In 1937 Brower's job was eliminated, but his desire to be in the mountains had grown stronger. In 1939 he worked part time in San Francisco in the office of the Sierra Club. This still left him with time for hiking, and in October of 1939 he led the first ascent of New Mexico's Ship Rock, then considered the most difficult climb in America.

The Sierra Club was then involved in the battle to have Kings Canyon in the Sierra preserved as a national park and it was Brower's initiation into conservation activism. By now he understood clearly what the threats to wilderness were. In the *Sierra Club Bulletin* he wrote:

> *Wilderness destruction proceeds on a one-way road. From mile to mile the course of destruction may seem justifiable enough. But when the road's end is reached, there is no turning back. The wilderness is gone, and with it the values of the primeval places to civilization— values that cannot be stated in dollars.*

He was involved in the making of the Sierra Club movie *Sky-Land Trails of the Kings,* filmed largely during the Sierra Club High

Trips of 1939 and 1940. This film was shown throughout California to raise support for preservation of this beautiful wilderness. This and other Sierra Club activities helped result in the creation of Kings Canyon National Park in 1940.

In 1941 he was hired as an editor by the University of California Press. There he met and shared an office with fellow editor Anne Hus. After the United States entry into World War II, Brower enlisted in the U.S. Mountain Troops. He was sent to officer school and then stationed in Colorado, where he taught mountain-climbing skills to other soldiers, taking time out to marry Hus on May 1, 1943. Shortly after their first child, Kenneth, was born, Brower was sent overseas. In the mountains of northern Italy, he experienced some of the horror of war, losing a number of friends and colleagues to enemy fire. When the war in Italy ended in 1945, he and his friends celebrated by skiing and climbing in the Alps.

In an article he wrote for the Sierra Club, Brower described his disappointment with what he saw: "In such parts of the mountains . . . as I have been able to observe, are the shattered remains of what must have been beautiful wildernesses. . . . Apparently men sought to cure the ills they thought the wilderness suffered from," such ills as "cliffs too high," or "streams too wide." He would later recall, "Those mountains punched so full of holes . . . strengthened my desire to protect the places in the Sierra Nevada."

Soon Brower was back at work, editing for the University of California Press, and editing the *Sierra Club Bulletin* on a volunteer basis as well. Over the years he and Anne became parents of three more children, Robert, Barbara, and John, each of whom they delighted in introducing to the wilderness.

He also continued to participate in as many of the Sierra Club's activities as he could, somehow managing to get time off from the press to lead Sierra Club High Trips. Articles he wrote in the *Bulletin* helped preserve the San Gorgonio Wild Area in California and old growth forests in Olympic National Park, add new units to the national park system, and establish the National Wilderness Preservation System.

In the early 1950s, the U.S. Bureau of Reclamation proposed the building of dams along the Colorado River and its tributaries to produce electricity. Known as the Colorado River Storage Project, the plan included dams at Flaming Gorge, Echo Park, Split Mountain, and Glen Canyon. Two of these, Echo Park and Split Mountain, were on the Green River in Dinosaur National

*The Green and Yampa rivers wind through Dinosaur National Monument.
Brower fought hard against the construction of dams in the monument.*
(Courtesy of National Park Service, HFC Historic Collection)

Monument which, besides dinosaur fossils, included 100 miles of canyons along the Green and Yampa rivers in northwestern Colorado.

This threatened invasion of the National Park System called to mind the Hetch Hetchy disaster and aroused the Sierra Club and other conservation organizations to fight it. In 1952 the Sierra Club hired David Brower as its first full-time executive director. His first task was to spearhead its campaign against the dams.

Brower realized that people who saw the beauty of Dinosaur would be more likely to protect it. Up to that point Dinosaur had not been heavily visited, except by geologists and paleontologists interested in the fossils that had been found in another part of the monument. He hired guides and boats to take 200 people on trips through the scenic canyons. Newspaper reporters, politicians, concerned citizens, all were encouraged to take a look, to see for themselves what a dam would destroy.

In testimony before a House Committee in January 1954, Brower described a journey through Dinosaur as the greatest scenic experience he'd ever had (a lofty compliment from a Californian who'd "grown up" in the Sierra Nevada). He claimed that his sons and many others who'd been there agreed. Brower went on to say that these scenic vistas would be destroyed with the building of dams in the monument's canyons.

One of the strongest parts of the anti-dam argument was a Charles Eggert film, *Wilderness River Trail,* made on one of those river trips, and Brower's movie, *Two Yosemites.* Brower's film showed the destruction caused by the damming of Hetch Hetchy and pleaded that this not be the fate of Dinosaur. Another effective weapon was a book called *This Is Dinosaur,* which Brower directed through publication and into the hands of the members of Congress.

When the time came for a vote in Congress, Brower was told by the Sierra Club's executive committee that if the Echo Park and Split Mountain dams were excluded from the proposal, the Sierra Club would not object to the rest of the project. Thus, the dams in Dinosaur would not be built, but the ones in Flaming Gorge and Glen Canyon would.

Brower allowed this to happen, much to his later regret. Between the time the bill was passed and the dams begun, he would get to know Glen Canyon and became very sorry that he had not fought for it as well. Glen Canyon had a hundred magnificent side canyons that, it was discovered too late, would be ruined when the dam was built.

In the foreword to the book *The Place No One Knew,* published in 1963, Brower wrote,

Glen Canyon died in 1963 and I was partly responsible for its needless death. So were you. Neither you nor I, nor anyone else, knew it well enough to insist that at all costs it should endure. When we began to find out, it was too late. . . . In Glen Canyon the people never knew what the choices were. Next time, in other stretches of the Colorado, on other rivers that are still free, and wherever there is wildness that can be part of our civilization instead of victim to it, the people need to know before a bureau's elite decide to wipe out what no one can replace. . . . With support from people who care, we hope in the years to come to help deter similar ravages of blind progress.

Out of the mistake that allowed the damming of Hetch Hetchy against John Muir's will came the National Park Act of 1916, which protected other beautiful places. Brower's hope was that by

When the U.S. Bureau of Reclamation proposed building dams in the Grand Canyon, Brower mounted a campaign against them that included full-page ads in national newspapers.
(Author's collection, photo by Robert O'Donnell)

showing what a mistake it was to dam Glen Canyon, some good would eventually come. He hoped that it would energize people to protect what was left of nature's wild, free places. It did steel Brower and other conservationists to prevent anything close to such destruction happening in the Grand Canyon itself when it too was threatened.

In the foreword to *Time and the River Flowing: Grand Canyon* (1964), Brower wrote: "Now the same bureau [that dammed Glen Canyon] has proposed to build dams in Grand Canyon itself as part of its Pacific Southwest Water Plan—to end the living river's flowing for all this civilization's time."

Between June 1966 and April 1967 the Sierra Club placed four full-page ads in national and local papers to oppose construction of dams in the Grand Canyon. In one Brower wrote: "This time it's the Grand Canyon they want to flood. *The Grand Canyon.*" Another, alluding to the statement by a Bureau of Reclamation engineer that flooding the Grand Canyon would allow people in boats to get closer to the walls, said, "Should we also flood the Sistine Chapel so tourists can get nearer the ceiling?"

This was not the first time Brower was involved in placing conservation ads. In December 1965 an ad on behalf of the redwoods was run with little controversy. But in the case of the Grand Canyon, the Sierra Club was opposing an action that the presidential administration favored, and the federal government responded by immediately having the Internal Revenue Service (IRS) threaten the club's tax deductible status, and then actually revoking it six months later.

This could have been a severe blow to the Sierra Club's fund-raising abilities, costing them hundreds of thousands of dollars in major contributions. Fortunately, Brower had previously set up a separate Sierra Club Foundation to receive large gifts, and the general public responded with a huge increase in smaller, nondeductible contributions. Membership leapt from 39,000 in June 1966, to 78,000 in June 1969. Sympathy for the club, and thus for its causes, increased as people saw them as being bullied by the IRS for opposing a government proposal. More important, the Johnson administration withdrew its support for the proposal and the Grand Canyon dams were not built.

Meanwhile, Brower and the Sierra Club were busy fighting for the Earth on many other fronts as well. Through the production of a number of large, beautiful books, called exhibit format books, the Sierra Club became established as a leader in conservation publishing. Brower also initiated the selling of calendars and posters with photos from the books as a way to support the publishing projects. These pioneering innovations in conservation publishing would later be adopted by many other conservation groups.

In the early 1960s, Brower met Rachel Carson at a dinner in New York when she was being awarded the Audubon Medal. Later, Brower's wife and daughter accompanied him when Carson asked him to visit Muir Woods with her a few months before she died. Of the author of *Silent Spring* he would write: "She removed a veil that had concealed from me what the life force consists of, and how interrelated are all of us who share in it. For the first time I began to understand that some of the essential building blocks of life were the same in people as they were in the lesser creatures people decided to kill with poison."

Brower was also actively involved in the battle to save the giant redwoods of California, a fight that had been dear to the heart of John Muir nearly a century before. *The Last Redwoods* was published by the Sierra Club in 1962 to explain the need for a Redwood National Park at Redwood Creek in Northern California. A park was created there in 1968.

Besides overseeing book publishing (and he was involved in selecting topics and authors, in design, in advising printers, and in marketing), Brower could be found testifying at hearings, making conservation speeches, and overseeing administration of the club. He was one of the few leaders of a national conservation organization whose name was known to the general public. *Life* magazine called him "the country's number one working conservationist."

Though the Sierra Club was larger at the end of the 1960s than it had ever been before, all the controversy of the decade had taken its toll on the organization. The club had become divided over

Like John Muir, his predecessor in the Sierra Club, Brower fought for the preservation of the redwood trees. Redwood National Park, where visitors like those shown here can enjoy the redwoods, was created in 1968.
(Courtesy of National Park Service, HFC Historic Collection)

both tactics and mission. Some of its long-standing members were concerned that the publishing program was draining the club's funds and blamed Brower and his aggressive tactics.

Then, early in 1969 Brower spent $10,000 on an ad in the *New York Times* that urged "treating the earth as a conservation district in the universe, sort of an Earth National Park." It was part of his plan for the Sierra Club to have a more global focus. Many members of the board of directors were extremely upset by Brower's seeming independence in the use of funds.

It seemed that the very characteristics that made Brower just right for the conservation cause in the 1960s—his aggressive style and willingness to question government decisions—made many of the directors of the Sierra Club uneasy. The showdown came over the choice of a site for a nuclear reactor to be built along the Pacific coast. After months of argument over this issue, Brower and four other colleagues decided to run for positions on the board of directors to get the Sierra Club to take a stand against Diablo Canyon as a site for the reactor. When Brower and the others were defeated, he was forced to resign as executive director on May 3, 1969.

A month later, Brower became executive director of the John Muir Institute for Environmental Studies, which he had co-founded in 1968 to carry on studies the Sierra Club had declined to undertake. On July 11, 1969, he founded and was named president of Friends of the Earth and its subsidiary, the League of Conservation Voters.

He intended for Friends of the Earth (FOE) to do some of the things he'd been restrained from doing with the Sierra Club—to be more internationally focused, to be even more politically and legislatively active, and to continue to pursue publishing.

Brower continued to be involved in the publishing of a wide variety of books related to conservation, including more in the exhibit format. Publisher Ian Ballantine told Brower that he had "put together books that made people fall in love with places, that told them of the threats to those places, and explained what they could do about those threats." Friends of the Earth produced a journal, *Not Man Apart,* to which Brower contributed. He also published a series of books with Earth Island Ltd. This was an organization he had founded in London to help support Friends of the Earth in Britain. Separate Friends of the Earth sister groups had been established in more than 50 countries.

When Brower learned that Senator Gaylord Nelson was organizing Earth Day, a day to honor the Earth and educate people about environmental issues, for April 22, 1970, Brower coordinated publication of a book called *The Environmental Handbook* to be in bookstores by that January. It provided concerned individuals with information on what they could do to help the Earth. It sold over a million copies.

When some members of the media (excepting the *New York Times,* which had long been conservation's friend) insisted on calling the public's aroused interest in the environment after Earth Day a "fad," he said, "I hope the media . . . having just discovered the environment, will stop calling the present interest in the environment a fad. It is not a fad unless survival is a fad."

Throughout the 1970s, as conservationism grew and expanded into environmentalism, Brower was there, speaking on behalf of Friends of the Earth and continuing to express himself in writing in the forewords of numerous books. There were now thousands of members in Friends of the Earth around the world.

He continued to see that the environment was a global issue, lobbying for "world heritage" sites, an expansion of the national park concept. This was a program that had been adopted by the United Nations in 1972 to protect Earth's outstanding natural and cultural areas. Brower had a hand in the development of a list of some 100 natural areas around the globe that merited world heritage protection. Books on the Galapagos Islands and Mount Everest helped those places attain such status.

In 1979 he retired as paid president of Friends of the Earth, and became the unpaid chairman. In 1984 he resigned from the board of the organization in protest over drastic program cuts, but he remained a member.

In the meanwhile, in 1982 he had founded Earth Island Institute. He wanted this to be an organization that would be involved in creative ways in a number of environmental campaigns, and it continues today in that work.

The general goal of Earth Island is to bring ecological conscience into all aspects of human activity. It is supporting a Global Restoration Fair to be held in San Francisco in 1995. Some of its current programs include the International Marine Mammals project, the Fate of the Earth conferences, the Urban Habitat Program, and the Global CPR Service (in this case, CPR stands for conservation, protection, and restoration). The Rainforest

David Brower

Action Network is a program that began as part of Earth Island but is now separately incorporated.

His interest in all of these projects keeps Brower a busy man. He travels frequently and continues to speak on behalf of the environment. One of his favorite talks these days is titled "It's Healing Time on Earth." He still loves the Sierra Nevada, and he and Anne, after 50-plus years of marriage, spend as much time there as they can. They have a favorite place there, well off the beaten path, that they call "Browers' Bench."

At the heart of all that David Brower is and does is wilderness—the exploration, the enjoyment, the protection of wild places and their natural inhabitants. Time and time again he has declared that "wilderness will not set itself aside." That is something we will have to do. And if we don't, it will be gone. And once it's gone, it will be gone forever.

In one of the first forewords written by Brower, for the magnificent book *This Is the American Earth*, published in 1960 (and again in 1992), he wrote:

> *Again and again, the challenge to explore has been met, handled, and relished by one generation—and precluded to any other. Although Thomas Jefferson argued that no one generation has a right to encroach upon another generation's freedom, the future's right to know the freedom of wilderness is going fast. And it need not go at all. A tragic loss could be prevented if only there could be a broader understanding of this: that the resources of the earth do not exist just to be spent for the comfort, pleasure, or convenience of the generation or two who first learn how to spend them; that some resources exist for saving, and what diminishes them, diminishes all mankind; that one of these is wilderness . . . that this, wilderness, is worth saving for what it can mean to itself as part of the conservation ethic; that the saving is imperative to civilization and all mankind, whether or not all men yet know it.*

In another place he wrote: "If what wilderness we have is left to serve its highest purpose—being there for itself and its indigenous life forms, being there as the outside to a world that is otherwise a cage, being there for its wholeness, its beauty, its truth—then those who understand it must speak again as lucidly and as persuasively as did Aldo Leopold, Robert Marshall, and Howard Zahniser." You could easily add the name of David Brower to that list.

Chronology

July 1, 1912	David Brower is born in Berkeley, California
1933	joins the Sierra Club
1935	first article published in the *Sierra Club Bulletin;* joins the editorial board; goes to work in Yosemite
1939–40	films *Sky-Land Trails of the Kings,* which is used in promoting creation of Kings Canyon National Park
1942–45	serves with U.S. Mountain Troops
May 1, 1943	marries Anne Hus
1945	returns to U.S. and Sierra Club activities
1952	hired by Sierra Club as first full-time executive director; fights against dams in Dinosaur National Monument
1969	resigns as executive director of Sierra Club; founds Friends of the Earth and the League of Conservation Voters
1979	retires as paid president of Friends of the Earth; stays on as unpaid chairman for five more years
1982	founds Earth Island Institute; remains active in many of its programs to promote an ecological conscience among humans
1992	*This Is the American Earth* revised edition published with updated foreword by Brower

Further Reading

Works by David Brower

For Earth's Sake. The Life and Times of David Brower (Salt Lake City, UT: Peregrine Smith Books, 1990). Brower describes people and events in his life that shaped and directed his commitment to working for the Earth.

Work in Progress (Salt Lake City, UT: Peregrine Smith Books, 1991). Part II of Brower's autobiography.

Other Works

Anker, Debby and John deGraaf. *David Brower, Friend of the Earth* (New York: Twenty-First Century Books, 1993). Biography for schoolchildren.

McPhee, John. *Encounters with the Archdruid* (New York: Farrar, Straus & Giroux, 1971). The author spent extensive amounts of time with Brower during the height of his leadership with the Sierra Club. Much of the book was first published in The New Yorker.

Turner, Tom. *Sierra Club. 100 Years of Protecting Nature* (New York: Harry N. Abrams, Inc., 1991). A history of the Sierra Club, including Brower's years of participation and leadership.

Gaylord Nelson:
Honoring the Earth

Gaylord Nelson.
(Courtesy of the Wilderness Society)

*I*n February 1969, there was an oil spill off the coast of Santa Barbara, California. Hundreds of thousands of gallons of oil washed ashore, coating the beaches and coastal wildlife. Pelicans, ducks, fish, and sea lions floundered in the muck and died.

On a summer's day a few months later, Gaylord Nelson, U.S. senator from Wisconsin, visited the site of the disaster. He'd been invited to Santa Barbara to speak at a conference on water and wanted to see for himself the damage caused by the oil slick.

What he saw distressed him greatly, and he was still thinking about it when he flew from Santa Barbara to Berkeley to speak at a conservation conference. While on the plane he read an article about student demonstrations called "teach-ins" being held on college campuses around the country. They used speeches, classes, and other activities to educate people about the Vietnam War.

Nelson knew that it was human activities that were causing the environmental crisis in America and believed that people had to be educated about harmful activities and taught alternatives. "I suddenly thought," Nelson would later recall, "why not have a national teach-in on the environment?"

From this brainstorm would come one of the largest demonstrations in U.S. history. Organized by Nelson and a corps of volunteers, the first Earth Day, April 22, 1970, drew the participation of some 20 million people. It was not, however, the first time Gaylord Nelson had spoken up on behalf of the environment; nor would it be the last.

Gaylord Nelson was born on June 4, 1916, in the small Wisconsin town of Clear Lake. Tucked in the northwest corner of the state, far from any large cities, Clear Lake was then a community of 700 people, surrounded by wilderness. At one end of Main Street was a marsh, inhabited by birds and muskrats. Nearby were several small, clear lakes created by ancient glaciers, and tall forests of pine, maple, and birch.

"There was a special adventure to being a young boy in northwestern Wisconsin," Nelson would later write. "There was the adventure of exploring a deep green pine forest, crunching noisily through the crisp leaves and pine needles on a fall day, or taking a cool drink from a fast running trout stream or a hidden lake." Throughout his boyhood Gaylord spent as much time as he could outdoors—swiming, fishing, and ice skating. "There was never any reason to believe that the rest of the world wasn't as clean and comfortable," an older and wiser Nelson would one day admit. "It was easy for the children of Clear Lake to believe that the legacy they had inherited in rich land, clean air, and safe water was one every boy and girl in the nation had."

When Gaylord was inside, he was more than likely reading. ("Everything I could get my hands on; that's what I read," he says.) Another popular activity in the Nelson house was political debate. Gaylord's father, Anton Nelson, was mayor of Clear Lake for a time while Gaylord was young, and his mother, Mary Bradt

Nelson, was also involved in public service. Local, state, and national politics provided interesting topics for neighborhood and family discussion.

Gaylord enjoyed accompanying his father on his rounds as a country doctor and at first he thought he'd like to help people in that way when he grew up. But when he was 10 years old he heard the Progressive politician "Fighting" Bob LaFollette speak from a train platform to a large, enthusiastic crowd, and he realized that politicians can help people too. Gaylord decided that he would become a politician and solve problems too. He thought he'd start by asking the village board to plant elm trees along the main entry into Clear Lake. The board members listened politely to the young boy's request, but they did not plant any trees.

After graduating from high school in Clear Lake, Nelson attended San Jose State College in California, and then returned to Wisconsin to attend the University of Wisconsin Law School. After receiving his law degree in 1942, Nelson spent four years in the U.S. Army.

When his term in the army ended in 1946, Nelson ran for the Wisconsin State Assembly. The race was close, but Nelson lost by a narrow margin. The next year he married Carrie Lee Dotson, an army nurse he'd met in the service. They settled in Madison, the Wisconsin state capital, where Nelson went into law practice.

In 1948 he ran for the state Senate as a Democrat, and this time he won. At last he held a political post and had partially achieved his childhood goal. It still remained for him to use his position to help people, and he set out to fulfill that mission as well. He must have satisfied the electorate in that regard as he was re-elected in 1952 and again in 1956.

During this time the Nelsons had two children, Gaylord Jr. and Cynthia. Another son, Jeffrey, was born a few years later.

Nelson's influence in the state Democratic party grew to the point that he was nominated for governor in 1958. Wisconsin had not had a Democrat in the governor's mansion since 1932, but that was changed when Nelson was elected on November 4, 1958.

In many of the speeches Nelson made as governor he talked about his boyhood days in Clear Lake. By now he realized that not all children in the United States, not even all children in Wisconsin, grew up in such idyllic conditions. He pledged that he would do all he could to preserve what remained of Wisconsin's wilderness heritage.

When Nelson was re-elected in 1960, he initiated a ten-year program of wilderness preservation. Under this program, $50 million was spent to purchase one million acres of privately owned land and convert it to publicly owned wilderness areas for recreation and wildlife habitat. It was a progressive program and placed Wisconsin in the forefront in state initiatives for conservation. Nelson was proud of this program, believing that it helped provide the opportunity for further generations of children to experience the peace and beauty of at least bits of wilderness.

By now he'd read the words of Aldo Leopold, who'd been a professor at the University of Wisconsin in Madison and had written much about wilderness. "I wish Leopold was still alive," said Nelson. "I'd put him in a job where he could do something." He read and reread *A Sand County Almanac* and worked hard to see that its wisdom was applied in Wisconsin.

Nelson also attacked the problem of detergent pollution. Many of the lakes and rivers around the nation were suddenly frothing with suds from detergents being dumped with sewage into waterways. After establishing a committee to study the problem, Nelson supported legislation that made Wisconsin one of the first states

As governor of Wisconsin, Nelson promoted the purchase of wilderness areas across the state, and supported legislation to halt pollution so that these areas would remain clean enough to be enjoyed.
(Courtesy of the Wilderness Society)

to regulate detergent pollution. He also signed into law restrictions on trash dumping and littering.

In 1962 Nelson decided to carry his program to the national level. In that year he ran for and won a seat in the U.S. Senate. Unlike other candidates, he talked a lot about the environment during the campaign, and he continued to discuss the issue even after election.

On March 25, 1963, in his first speech before the U.S. Senate, Nelson focused on the environment. "We need a comprehensive and nationwide program to save the national resources of America," he said. "We cannot be blind to the growing crisis of our environment. Our soil, our water, and our air are becoming more polluted every day. Our most priceless natural resources—trees, lakes, rivers, wildlife habitats, scenic landscapes—are being destroyed." He immediately made it clear that he supported a nationwide ban on nonbiodegradable detergents.

He also listened to what people had to say about the environment. He heard many older people speaking sadly of favorite childhood nature spots that were now either badly polluted or converted into shopping malls and parking lots.

As he listened he saw the connections between the stories. He saw that many of the environment's problems had grown too big for local and state governments to handle alone. He saw what he called "the awful dimensions of the catastrophes."

When other politicians asked him why he kept talking about the environment he said, "Because people care." But his remained a lonely voice in the political arena. Neither presidential candidates nor senators or members of Congress wanted to talk about it. Nelson figured that in 1963 probably only about 20 of the 535 members of Congress would have called themselves environmentalists. As late as 1968 Nelson did not hear a single speech on the environment given by a presidential candidate.

Still, Nelson continued to work on behalf of the environment. In 1963 he convinced President John Kennedy to make a "resource and conservation" tour of the United States. He hoped that this would draw national media attention to the environment. Of course he made sure that the president's trip would include a stop in northern Wisconsin. When he viewed some of the undeveloped land that had been set aside for future generations in Nelson's home state, Kennedy praised the efforts saying, "What has been done here must be done in every state in the country."

Reporters did not seem to think that this was big news, however, for it did not get much attention in the national press. A few weeks later, Kennedy was assassinated and Lyndon Johnson became president. Nelson continued to try to find support for his environmental initiatives.

Thus the problems of the environment weighed heavy on his mind as he visited the Santa Barbara coast in August 1969, and as he flew on to Berkeley. The idea he had in flight, that perhaps a teach-in on the environment was called for, was an idea that would spark a resurgence in environmentalism. It would provide individuals across the country with the opportunity to say "we care" in a voice loud enough to be heard.

When Nelson arrived in Berkeley, he mentioned his idea to some of the students and teachers he talked to, and their response was enthusiastic. He returned to Washington after the conference was over and announced his plan in the Senate. "The youth of today face an ugly world of the future," he said, "with dangerously and deadly polluted air and water. I am proposing a national teach-in on the crisis of the environment."

He began raising funds and recruiting people to help him, though he was not yet sure exactly what form this "teach-in" would take. He sent letters to the governors of all the states and to the mayors of major cities, asking them to issue Earth Day Proclamations. He wrote an Earth Day article to appear in college newspapers and *Scholastic* magazine. A few weeks later he gave a speech in Seattle, Washington, in which he announced that on April 22, 1970, there would be "an event in honor of the earth," that on this day people would be able "to present the facts about our environment clearly and dramatically."

Before he could make it back to Washington, D.C., the phones in his office were ringing with people calling to see how they could help. "It was the grass-roots support that made it," says Nelson. "With it you can do anything—without it, nothing."

A young law student named Denis Hayes was one of those who volunteered to help handle inquiries. He managed the national office that was set up as a clearing house for information. Thousands of colleges, high schools, and elementary schools planned their own activities. Says Nelson, "We had neither the time nor resources to organize the ten thousand grade schools and high schools and one thousand communities that participated. They simply organized themselves. That was the remarkable thing about Earth Day."

Gaylord Nelson

Finally the preparations were all made and the day for the festivities drew near. Congress was adjourned so that the people's representatives could learn along with their constituents about environmental problems.

On the evening before Earth Day, Nelson was in Madison, Wisconsin. Speaking before a large crowd he said

> *Earth Day can be the birth date of a new way of thinking that says "This land was not put here for us to use up." Earth Day can be the beginning of a way of thinking that says, "Even a country as rich as ours must depend on the natural systems that preserve the air, the water, and the land." The future can be preserved only if we change, only if we change our attitudes toward nature and nature's works. . . . It will take a commitment far beyond any effort ever made before.*

He asked the rhetorical question, "Are we able to do this?" and answered emphatically, yes. "But are we *willing* to do this?" he continued. "That's the unanswered question."

When April 22 dawned on the United States, very nearly every town had planned some sort of recognition of Earth Day. There were marches and concerts, nature walks and picnics. In some places streets were blocked off to encourage people to walk. In many places trees were planted and litter was picked up.

It is estimated that some 20 million Americans participated in Earth Day events, making it one of the largest one-day demonstrations in this nation's history. Nelson himself was a little bit surprised at the response generated by his call for an Earth Day. "I knew it would be a big event," he said, "but it was even bigger than I thought."

Nelson was extremely heartened by the huge success of Earth Day. "Across America," he said, "there is a disgust, a rising anger, a demand for action. Earth Day demonstrates the widespread concern for a livable world. It makes me believe for the first time that we can wage a successful fight to save the earth."

Earth Day may have been a one-day demonstration, but it was to spark many, many days of activity. When the speeches and classes were over, it was time for people to go to work. "We need action," said Nelson. "We need political action nationwide to restore the quality of our environment."

Suddenly politicians were talking about the environment. This was just what Nelson had hoped for. "My major objective in planning Earth Day was to organize a nationwide public demonstration so large it would finally get the attention of the politicians and force the environmental issue into the political dialogue of the nation," says Nelson. "It worked," he adds.

Across the nation an educated pubic was taking its concerns to government. New laws were passed regulating chemical pesticide use. Cleanup programs for air and waterways were introduced. The Environmental Protection Agency (EPA) was established to see that these cleanups took place. Nelson sponsored the Water Quality Act, which sought to end the dumping of toxic wastes in the world's oceans, and the National Lakes Preservation Act, which would begin cleanup of badly polluted lakes. In November 1971, *Environmental Quality* magazine called Nelson "the leading environmentalist in the U.S. Senate."

Preservation of wilderness areas continued to be one of Nelson's priorities. Mountain slopes and river shores were priceless resources as endangered as the air and water and wildlife. Nelson was instrumental in the development of a federally protected nation-wide system of hiking trails, including the 2,000-mile-long Appalachian Trail and the Pacific Crest Trail, which winds through the western mountains from Canada to Mexico. Of course, northern Wisconsin was never far from his thoughts, and he was pleased to have the Ice Age Trail included in the system, preserving some of the rugged terrain carved by glaciers long ago.

He deplored the continuing pressure of development on fields and marshlands. He once had his staff figure out how many miles of American land were paved with highways. The figure came out to be 76,000 square miles, enough to cover the entire state of Wisconsin plus 20,000 square miles more.

For 18 years he served as a senator from Wisconsin, fighting for the environment from start to finish. In 1980 he was defeated in a bid for re-election to a fourth term. Though he had been prepared to serve again, he accepted defeat as an inevitable part of political life. His children were grown and he looked forward to spending time with them and their children. And he found that he could continue to fight for the environment as counselor of the Wilderness Society, the organization co-founded by Aldo Leopold, the conservationist he so admired. In 1982 he was presented with the "Environmental Leadership Award" by the United Nations Environmental Programme (UNEP).

As the 20th anniversary of the first Earth Day approached, people looked around and took stock of all that had occurred. There had been some improvements, but in many places, things had gotten worse. A group of people (including Denis Hayes, who had worked so hard on the first Earth Day) went to work organizing Earth Day 1990. They came up with the motto "Think Globally, Act Locally" to show that this Earth Day was for all the world. Gaylord Nelson was asked to be honorary chairman. Again he was called upon to make speeches and urge action.

He remembered when he had first realized that environmental problems were too big for local governments to handle alone. Now he knew that even the federal government was not big enough. He called for an attitude of "environmental citizenship," for Americans to think of themselves as citizens of Earth as well as of the United States. That took care of the "global" part.

Millions of people stepped forward to carry out the "local" part. Recycling centers were established in many cities. People were encouraged to separate materials such as glass, plastic, aluminum, and paper from their other garbage so that they could be recycled into new materials. Not only would this save on energy and raw materials, it would help alleviate the problem of landfills overflowing with waste.

As counselor for the Wilderness Society, Nelson continues to work on behalf of the wilderness areas of our country. He believes that all children have the right to inherit "rich land, clean air, and safe water."
(Courtesy of the Wilderness Society)

Schoolchildren planted trees and picked up garbage. Environmental education was added to the curriculum of many schools. Many people decided that Earth Day should be an annual occurrence so that people will not forget how important it is to change our attitude and our behavior toward the Earth. On Earth Day 1992, Nelson was again honored by the United Nations Environmental Programme, this time with the "Only One Earth Award."

It is not an accident that much of the Earth Day activity takes place in schools. Nelson has great hopes that with sufficient education the next generation may be the "conservation generation so vital to our future." He wants to see environmental education taught in all the elementary and high school classrooms. He believes that this is the only way we will have citizens with the knowledge and the ethics to face the difficult decisions ahead.

He hopes that some of the children thus educated will become political leaders. Of Bill Clinton and Al Gore he says, "We finally have both a president and a vice-president deeply concerned about and strongly committed to the environment." He adds that "presidential leadership [in environmental issues] is not merely important—it is crucial."

Looking back over the years since that first Earth Day, Nelson says, "There are more people who care each year and they know far more than they used to know. The most important difference is that fewer and fewer people hold to the old belief that the world is too huge to be damaged by us."

Nelson has helped educate the people of the United States about the environment, and, as he told a reporter for *Mother Jones* magazine, "I'm now thinking about a worldwide demonstration that forces this issue onto the agenda of politicians all over the world." To help make that vision a reality, he has been named chairman of Earth Day U.S.A. for the 25th anniversary of Earth Day in 1995. Millions of people across the United States and tens of millions worldwide are expected to participate. Never content with what has already been done, Nelson continues to deliver speeches entitled "Where Do We Go From Here?"

Chronology

June 4, 1916	Gaylord Nelson is born in Clear Lake, Wisconsin
1942	graduates from University of Wisconsin Law School; enters the U.S. Army
1946	discharged from army; loses bid for election to Wisconsin State Assembly
1947	marries Carrie Lee Dotson; enters law practice in Madison, Wisconsin
1948	elected to Wisconsin Senate
1958	elected governor of Wisconsin
1960	initiates purchase of wilderness areas
1962	elected to the U.S. Senate
1969	calls for a national "teach-in" on the environment
April 22, 1970	Earth Day, an "event to honor the Earth" is held
1970–1980	Nelson works for passage of environmental cleanup and wilderness preservation legislation
1980	defeated in bid for re-election; becomes counselor of the Wilderness Society
1982	honored with "Environmental Leadership Award" by UNEP
April 22, 1990	serves as honorary chair, Earth Day 1990
1992	honored with "Only One Earth Award" by UNEP
1993	prepares to chair Earth Day U.S.A. to recognize 25th anniversary of Earth Day in 1995

Further Reading

Works by Gaylord Nelson

"The Environmental Challenge—Where Do We Go From Here?" Speech given by Nelson as Counselor of the Wilderness Society, at the Institute of Scrap Recycling Industries, Inc., March 13, 1992. Describes changes in behavior that must be made to conserve our resource base and achieve a sustainable economy.

"Brief History of Earth Day." Short description of the development of Earth Day. Includes a quote from the *New York Times* about Earth Day, and an excerpt from Nelson's speech at the University of Wisconsin, April 21, 1970.

Other works

Lowery, Linda. *Earth Day* (Minneapolis, MN: Carolrhoda Books, 1991). Written for very young students. A short, clear explanation of the origins of the first Earth Day and why we continue to honor it.

Shulman, Jeffrey and Teresa Rogers. *Gaylord Nelson, A Day for the Earth* (Frederick, MD: Twenty-First Century Books, 1992). Biography for schoolchildren. Describes Nelson's youth in Clear Lake, Wisconsin, his political career, and his concern for the environment every step of the way.

Index

Numbers in **boldface** indicate main headings; numbers in *italics* indicate illustrations.

Index

Index

149

Index